The Children's Minister

The Children's Minister

Rita B. Hays

DISCIPLESHIP RESOURCES

P.O. BOX 340003 • NASHVILLE, TN 37203-0003
www.discipleshipresources.org

ISBN 978-0-88177-527-3
Library of Congress Control Number 2008920847

To my sons, Allen and Ben,
and to the children who have
known me as pastor

CONTENTS

INTRODUCTION

A myriad of books have been written to help pastors develop programming for children. These "how to" books are very helpful, making it easy for the busy children's pastor or children's committee to plan year-round programming for children. There are books on establishing a children's ministry team, books on seasonal activities for children, and books on events for children based on the church year. Books have been written for every age-level of child, with details on the physical, mental, social, and spiritual development of children at each stage. Materials have been provided on how to establish a quality nursery and how to set up and administer a church-led daycare or parent's day out program. Numerous books have been written to deal with teacher training for those who volunteer to work with children in the church. Easy-to-use programs and curriculum have been developed for Sunday school, Vacation Bible school, Wednesday night programming, and Sunday evening children's clubs. As a pastor to children I already have many of these publications on my bookshelf.

One resource was missing, however. Nothing was available to help me be a pastor to children. I had a wealth of resources to help me plan programs, but nothing to help me connect with the lives of children. Where could I turn for help when a child faced a death in the family or a serious illness? What could I tell parents who asked me if it was appropriate for their child to attend Aunt Jane's funeral? How should I react when Bobby cried when telling me his dog had died? Was there anything I could do for Sue when I learned her parents were divorcing? These are pastoral concerns, and the answers to my questions could not be found in my numerous programming books. I needed answers to questions for which I had few resources to consult.

The lack of practical pastoral resources for children puzzled me. Part of this void may be the trend that is prevalent in churches today. We know that persons are drawn to our churches not by denominational labels so much as by quality programming. Many families with children relate that they choose their church home primarily by what the church has to offer the children and families. Good children's programming is at the top of the list for most families today when they are selecting their church. So it is obvious that we need books and resources to help us plan quality programming for children.

Yet I believe that there may be a deeper truth to our lack of pastoral resources. Pastors may not perceive their role as being a pastor to children. Many have not even thought about the need to pastor children in the church. Some pastors have believed that if they were a pastor to the adults or to the family, they had fulfilled their ministerial duties. Children have been overlooked because of our failure to realize they, too, need a pastor. Children yearn to be recognized as persons of worth. They want pastors to know them individually and be aware of what is happening in their lives.

Those who work with children in church settings, be it paid staff workers, children's pastors, directors of children's ministries, or volunteers, have been content with planning and carrying out numerous programs to reach children and draw them into the life of the church. These persons have never taken the opportunity to *pastor* children. Then when a crisis arises, they lack the know-how to minister to children. Senior pastors have often designated paid staff persons as the ones who should interact with children, thus senior pastors have neglected to relate to children as their pastor. And even in churches where the pastor had no paid staff to help with age-level programming, the pastor has often been unable to communicate with children and meet their pastoral needs.

Part of our problem stems from the fact that we are not even aware of the crises that children go through. What a child may perceive as a great need may not have even occurred to an adult. Identifying these concerns is helpful, but again there were very few resources for pastors to apply. Even in situations where pastors, staff, and volunteers have earnestly sought to minister to children, many have felt incompetent to deal with children.

Many situations arise where pastors feel inadequate to minister to the children. One of these is in the area of visitation. When a pastor visits a home where there are children present, there is the tendency to ignore the children. Many pastors relate that even if they wish to communicate with the children, they do not know what to say or how to talk with children. Most pastors have not even thought of making a personal visit to the children in the home. Then, there are the times in which children are hospitalized; pastors may enter the hospital room relaxed and positive when visiting an adult, but that same pastor enters the room with fear and intimidation when visiting a child.

This book is written from over twenty years of ministry with children: visiting in their homes, caring for them and their pets, being a pastor to them in times of crises, celebrating with them the joy of special events, and walking with them in the ordinary events of life. My focus is on pastoral care needs for children. Practical guidelines are given, and recommended books are listed.

Chapter one explores the important role of mentors in a child's life. The pastor to children is challenged to see himself or herself as a mentor to children and also involve other adult mentors within the congregation. Detailed information is presented on how to set up an adopted grandparent program, which offers children support and mentoring from their church family.

Chapter two offers practical advice on how to visit children in the home. Included in this chapter are ways to converse with children and methods to set up a visitation program.

Chapter three helps pastors recognize the importance of pets. Ideas are given for ministry when a pet dies, and a Blessing of the Animals service is provided for an intergenerational service.

Chapter four deals with the many crises that children may face. Examples include a new baby, divorce, adoption, child abuse, and violence. Other life events are discussed, such as moving to a new city.

Chapter five gives practical, in-depth resources for ministering to children coping with death. Suggestions are provided for pastors and parents who talk with children about death, and guidelines are included for children attending funerals and visitation.

Chapter six strengthens the pastor's ability to minister to children in times of illness or in times when a parent is ill. There are sections dealing with chronically ill children and terminally ill children.

Chapter seven provides the pastor with ideas for helping children celebrate birthdays and special occasions. There are sections relating to secular holidays and the church seasons. Details are given on how to remember children on their birthdays.

This book is recommended for senior pastors, church staff, children's pastors, and directors of children's ministries in local churches. Volunteers, such as Sunday school teachers and children's committee members, will also find the book helpful.

Jesus blessed the children and gave them a place of priority in the kingdom of God. We bless children when we focus our attention on them, offering the presence of Christ. We teach a powerful lesson to our congregations when we give children a place of priority in our busy schedules. We let others know that "the least of these" are worthy of our love, care, and time. (Matthew 25:45) My earnest prayer is that this book will relieve you of some of the anxiety you may feel when being a pastor to children. I hope it will also let you know that there is no greater calling than lifting up children in your ministry, saying by your words and actions that children are valued. So, go to talk with children, sit with children, cry with children, and laugh with children. See your task not as a burden but as a joy. The children are waiting for you. Go as their pastor!

CHAPTER ONE

"I Have An Adopted Grandparent!"

·❖· *The Role of Mentors in the Life of Children* ·❖·

One of the most joyful occasions for a family and for a congregation is the birth of a child. Churches are discovering the importance of welcoming the child into the life of the congregation. The pastor may visit the newborn in the hospital and a rose may be placed on the altar to celebrate the birth of a newborn. At the baptism or dedication of a child, depending on one's tradition, the congregation will be asked to take a vow along with the parents. Usually this vow is a promise of the church family to help raise the child in the Christian faith. The congregation should take this vow very seriously. It involves their commitment to be a part of the lives of children in their midst. The members of the faith community have declared that they will become mentors for the children.

This understanding of the promise to participate in the lives of children and support the families in a congregation is the starting point for gathering support for the role of faith friends in the life of children. Any time people are recruited to work with children, they need to be reminded of this vow that was made at the baptism or dedication of a child. Children need many mentors to offer support and encouragement and to teach the faith stories. Children especially need the wisdom of older members of the congregation. Many children have grandparents that live distances from them. And regardless, children need contact with adult role models who are willing to take the time to share with them. The Adopt-a-Grandparent program is an excellent way for children, youth, and adults to be linked together for friendship and faith sharing.

The Adopt-a-Grandparent program is designed to bring children, youth, and adults together as friends and Christian mentors. Children and adults who agree to participate in the program are asked to sign up for this annual program. Children and adults may suggest persons they wish to adopt. After the program is set up and children and adults are matched, many intergenerational events may be planned to bring together persons who are a part of the Adopt-a-Grandparent program. Suggestions should also be given to persons on how to share one-on-one with the adopted grandparent or grandchild. The following pages will give instructions on how to set up the Adopt-a-Grandparent program, how to continue the program year after year, suggestions and guidelines for participants, and questions often asked about the program. Ideas will also be offered on fellowship and learning events churches may plan for the Adopt a Grandparent participants and well as church-wide intergenerational events, which give children the opportunity to invite their adopted grandparents to share with them.

Communication is essential in order to ensure the success of this program. Begin by sharing the idea for the Adopt-a-Grandparent program with the senior pastor and staff. Gather their support for this project and ask them to share with others the importance of the program. Promote the program in worship, the church newsletter, and bulletin. Begin to talk with leaders within the church and committees to gain their support. Of course, it is essential to talk with the senior adult groups, including Sunday school classes and any fellowship groups.

When you are ready to begin the program, send letters to families in the church with children and senior adults or "empty nesters" whom you might think would be good adopted grandparents. In your letter, enclose some information about the program as well as some questions and answers about the program. A sample of some of the questions that are often asked when beginning this program are enclosed with suggested answers, but each congregation will have their own concerns and questions. Answer these honestly so that persons understand exactly what the program is about and what is being expected of them. This will ensure that your program is successful year after year. In your letter, also include some ideas for the children and grandparents on activities and ways to remember one another on special occasions. You will also want to include a postcard where persons may sign up for the program, returning the card to the church. A sample of the letter to be sent, sign-up postcard, and ideas for the Adopt-a-grandparent program are enclosed.

Once persons have indicated any interest in the program, begin to match children/youth and adults together. Some children may indicate that they want the same adopted grandparent. When this happens, allow the child that has returned his or her postcard first to adopt this person. However, sometimes the adopted grandparents will agree to adopt more than one child. Siblings sometimes ask for the same adopted grandparent or each sibling may wish to have his or her own adopted grandparent. Some children will adopt a married couple; while in some cases, married couples wish to have his or her own adopted grandchild. Flexibility is a key to making this program work. There will be adults within the congregation who already have grandchildren who attend the church. Sometimes these persons are reluctant to become involved in the program since their grandchildren are present with them in the church community. Assure these persons that they are welcome to be involved in the program. Likewise, children who already have grandparents in your congregation are encouraged to participate since children need many mentors in the faith.

Inevitably, you will find that you have a larger list of children than adults when you begin recruiting for the program. Children seem to embrace this program, but some adults, at first, are reluctant to sign up. When children have listed an adult that they wish to adopt, but the adult have not indicated they want to be a part of the program, a phone call or conversation in person is helpful. Explain to the adult that a child in the church wishes to adopt them. Very often, the adult will agree to be a part of the program when they know that a child has selected them. Sometimes it is a matter of prayer and spiritual discernment on the part of the person who is matching the children and adults. This person has to be sensitive to the needs of all person involved. Sometimes it seems a challenge to try to bring together these children and adults to begin a friendship relationship. You will be amazed how often the Spirit of God will help you in your choices, and it is wonderful to hear the testimony of the adults after they have spent some time with the adopted grandchild.

Since this is a program in which the Children's Committee or other committees in the church will be planning several events throughout the year, it is not necessary for the adopted grandchildren and adopted grandparents to share in activities outside of the church. However, many adopted grandparents and children want to do so and are encouraged to do so if they are able. Adopted grandparents and grandchildren can share meals together. This might be as simple as going out to eat after church or having the adopted grandparent or grandchild in the home for a meal. Adopted grandparents could attend a function in which the child is involved, a sporting event, dance recital, music recital, or awards ceremony. However, this level of involvement is not necessary. Children and adopted grandparents might send each other cards on birthday and anniversaries. Children may bake or decorate a special card for the adopted grandparent. While individuals do not have to spend a lot of money in this program, sometimes children and adults wish to purchase one another gifts on special occasions such as birthdays, anniversaries, Christmas,

Valentine's Day, or other times throughout the year. This is left to the discretion of the adopted grandparents and families of the church. Yet, it is vital to let everyone know that it is not necessary to purchase monetary gifts for one another. This will be a concern for many senior adults on fixed incomes and families who have financial burdens. Do not let this concern keep them from participating in the program.

Lack of time is often a key factor that keeps some persons from wanting to participate in the program. Communicate with these persons that they do not have to spend time on activities outside of those planned by the church, unless they desire. They will be invited to participate in the intergenerational activities that will be planned during the year, but this is certainly not mandatory. Encourage these persons to share with one another during worship times and during events of the church family. For example, children and adults may sit together in worship and share Communion. Or they may attend fellowship events together. During the year, several events will be planned just for persons who are a part of the Adopt-a-Grandparent program. These events will provide ideal times for persons to share together, especially those who are unable to spend time outside of the church activities. Do not discourage persons from participating because they do not have time to spend together on activities outside of the church community.

Once you have matched the children and adults, you are ready to begin the program. Select a Sunday in your church as Adopt-a-Grandparent Sunday. Have a dedication service in the worship time, asking all of the adopted grandparents and children to come to the altar for a time of prayer and dedication. Offer an event after church or during Sunday school for fellowship. This will be a time for the adopted grandparents and children to get to know one another and see others who are participating in the program. Let the congregation know that they are able to sign up for these program at any time during the year.

The second year of the program and thereafter, you may ask certain persons to speak in the worship service or at other events to promote the program. These persons may share how meaningful the program has been to them.

The Children's Committee in your church and other groups may plan several events during the church year for persons who are a part of the Adopt-a-Grandparent Program. Occasions such as Valentine's Day, Grandparent's Day, and the Christmas season are all good times to plan special fellowship events. These times are designed to bring together only those persons in the church involved in the program and the families of the children. However, when the church plans intergenerational events that are open to the entire church family encourage children and adopted grandparents to attend together. This is also an opportunity to have children who do not have an adopted grandparent to invite a special friend or mentor in the church to attend with them. A list of some of the special occasions around which your congregation might plan Adopt-a-Grandparent gathering is included in this chapter, along with some ideas for intergenerational events.

What are the suggested ages of the children who participate in the program? That depends on the adopted grandparents and families of the children. Some adults wish to adopt babies in the congregation to support the young parents. Teenagers are encouraged to adopt a grandparent as well. Work with the Youth Director of Minister of Youth to invite the youth to be a part of this program. Sometimes youth will want to adopt homebound members of the congregation who are not able to come to the activities of the Adopt-a-Grandparent program, but are visited by the youth. As far as the adults involved in the program, try to begin with the senior adults in your congregation. However, often empty nesters are glad to be a part of the program.

The Adopt-a-Grandparent program is a continual event in the life of the congregation. On a designated date each year, ask people to sign up again for the program. Some children and adopted grandparents wish to keep the same persons because they have formed a special bond of friendship. Others will want to make changes. Some will want to drop out of the program. Honor these requests and recruit new persons to be a part of the program. Some churches decide that they want to have people change each year and select new adopted grandparents and grandchildren because this gives individuals an opportunity to get to know many mentors within the congregation. Discuss this with your planning committee to establish a policy before the program begins. However, you will find that it is often very difficult for children and adults to change to a new adopted grandparent/grandchild after they get to know one another and establish a relationship.

The wonderful part of this program is that adopted grandparents do not just establish a relationship with the children, but with the families of the children as well. Adopted grandparents may be asked to stand with families at the baptism of children, along with the grandparents and other family members. They will serve as Confirmation mentors, Sunday school teachers, Vacation Bible school leaders, or help with special events for children. This program strengthens the entire congregation as persons take seriously the calling to be mentors and faith friends for children in the faith community.

Starting an Adopt-a-Grandparent Program

1. Gain the support of your senior pastor, staff, Children's Committee and other groups within the church.
2. Begin to share with groups in the congregation through newsletters, committee meetings, fellowship gatherings, and during worship about the importance of the program. Use biblical examples of persons sharing the faith across generations.

Talk about the importance of the baptismal vows of the congregation, or in some denomination, the vows at the dedication of a child.

3. Share with the children about the program.

4. Select a Sunday to be designated Adopt-a-Grandparent Sunday. Begin to pray for the program and for the persons who will sign up to be a part of the program.

5. One month prior to the Sunday designated as Adopt-a-Grandparent Sunday, send a letter to children, senior adults, empty nesters, and other persons whom you feel would want to be a part of this program. Give them information about the program, have a question and answer pamphlet prepared, include suggestions for ways children and adults may share with one another in the program, and enclose a postcard for signing up for the program. The sign-up postcard should allow the option to list several persons to be adopted. Sometimes children and adults will have a strong preference for the person or persons they wish to be linked with. Try to honor these requests as much as possible. Some adults and children will want to participate in the program, but will need suggestions on persons they may adopt.

6. Call children and adults who have not signed up for the program. Share with them about program and urge them to consider being a part.

7. Meet with the Children's Committee or the committee designated to work on the Adopt-a-Grandparent program and begin to pair the adults with the children.

8. When you have children and adults who do not have someone to adopt, ask persons to volunteer for the program.

9. Contact participants by mail or phone to let them know their adopted grandparent or grandchild.

10. Promote the Adopt-a-Grandparent Sunday and invite people to participate. Plan a special day in worship with a fellowship event sometime during the day (during Sunday school, after worship, during the afternoon or evening). Adopted grandparents and children are asked to sit together in worship. During the service, have a time of dedication. A bulletin insert might list the names of the adopted grandparents and adopted grandchildren.

11. Plan special events throughout the year for the adopted grandparents and adopted grandchildren. Plan intergenerational events where all members of the church family may participate, but children will especially want to invite adopted grandparents to attend.

12. Encourage adopted grandparents and adopted grandchildren to remember one another on special occasions such as birthday, anniversaries, and holidays. It is not necessary to purchase a monetary gifts. Baked items, craft items, or handmade cards are appreciated.

13. Take pictures of adopted grandparents and adopted grandchildren and display in the church.

Sample Form (to be used the first year of the program)

Draft a letter to send to persons you feel would want to be a part of the Adopt-a-Grandparent program. Include examples of different scenarios, such as, "If your family has more than one child, we have enclosed a postcard for each child; however, if you wish to have the same adopted grandparent for all the children in your family, please indicate this to us. If you are an adult couple, please indicate to us if you wish to adopt the same child or children in a family or have separate adopted grandchildren. If you are a single adult, please indicate if you wish to adopt one grandchild or several grandchildren in a family, or several grandchildren from different families." Include with this letter the appropriate number of response postcards. (See sample below.)

ADOPT-A-GRANDPARENT SIGN UP

Please indicate below the names of a person or persons whom you wish to adopt for the Adopt-a-Grandparent program. We will do our very best to honor your request. If your first choice is also the first choice of other individuals, we will select based on who handed in the card first. **Please return this postcard to the church office.**

MY (OUR) NAME(S): _____

Please list three persons whom you might adopt:

1st choice: _____

2nd choice: _____

3rd choice: _____

_____ It does not matter to me. Please select for me an Adopt-a-Grandparent or Adopt-a-Grandchild who wishes to participate in the program.

Sample Form (to be used after the first year)

ADOPT-A-GRANDPARENT SIGN UP

MY (OUR) NAME(S): _____

_____ I currently have an adopted grandchild and would like to continue this wonderful relationship.

_____ I currently have an adopted grandparent and would like to continue this wonderful relationship.

_____ I currently have an adopted grandchild, but would not like to participate in the program this coming year.

_____ I currently have an adopted grandparent, but would not like to participate in the program this coming year.

_____ I currently have an adopted grandchild, but would like to have a new one assigned to me this year.

_____ I currently have an adopted grandparent, but would like to have a new one assigned to me this year.

_____ I do not currently have an adopted grandchild, but would like to participate in the program this year.

_____ I do not currently have an adopted grandparent, but would like to participate in the program this year.

I would like to adopt _____.

_____ Please assign me any adopted grandparent or grandchild who wishes to participate.

Sample Informational Form for Adopted Grandparent to give to Adopted Child

I HAVE AN ADOPTED GRANDCHHILD!

THE NAME OF MY ADOPTED GRANDPARENT(S) IS (ARE):

_____

ADDRESS:

_____

PHONE #S:

_____

BIRTHDAY(S)

_____

ANNIVERSARY DATE (If relevant):

_____

OCCUPATION & PLACE OF WORK
(If retired, what was your former occupation?):

_____

HOBBIES AND INTERESTS:

_____

OTHER THINGS I (WE) WISH TO SHARE WITH ADOPTED GRAND-
CHILD(REN):

_____

_____

Sample Form for Adopted Grandchild to Give to Adopted Grandparent(s)

I HAVE AN ADOPTED GRANDPARENT(S)!

Please fill out as and give to your adopted grandparent(s) as soon as possible. Thanks!

MY NAME IS: _____

MY ADDRESS & PHONE NUMBERS ARE: _____

_____

MY SCHOOL IS: _____

GRADE I AM IN: _____   MY AGE: _____

MY BIRTHDAY: _____

THINGS I LIKE TO DO (Hobbies, Sports, Fun Activities):

_____

MY FAVORITE COLOR(S) IS (ARE): _____

MY FAVORITE FOODS ARE: _____

OTHER THINGS YOU WOULD LIKE TO SHARE WITH YOUR ADOPTED GRANDPARENT(S): _____

_____

_____

Suggestions for Adopted Grandparents

1. Get to know the parents of your adopted grandchild. Ask them to offer suggestions for times to get together and share with you what the child/youth enjoys doing.
2. Remember the adopted grandchild on his/her birthday. It is not necessary to buy a gift. A card is appropriate. Children and youth also enjoy baked goods.
3. Remember the adopted grandchild on special holidays such as Christmas, Thanksgiving, Halloween, and Easter. A card or phone call is appropriate. A gift is not necessary. However, if you wish to purchase a small treat, children enjoy candy, baked goods, key chains, books, puzzles, and school items.
4. Call your adopted grandchild occasionally. Invite them to go with you out to eat. Most children and youth like pizza, hamburgers, and tacos. Get them to tell you their favorite places to eat. If you wish, invite them to your house to eat.
5. Sit with your adopted grandchild in church. It is not necessary to do this every Sunday. Communion is a good time to sit with your adopted grandchild and share this special time together.
6. Invite the adopted grandchild to your home. They might enjoy helping you with some chores such as raking leaves, planting flowers, or helping with Christmas decorations.
7. Take an interest in the activities of your adopted grandchild. It is not necessary to attend events outside of church, but if you wish to and are able to, you might attend some events such as sports, school recognition, school lunch, and dance/piano recitals. You might like to attend some community events such as children's plays, a parade, or a movie.
8. Remember the adopted grandchild when they have a death or illness in the family. The loss of a pet is a difficult time for children. Send them a card or talk with them on the phone.
9. Pray for your adopted grandchild each day.
10. Give your adopted grandchild a picture of you.

Suggestions for an Adopted Grandchild

1. Remember your adopted grandparent on special occasions such as his/her birthday and anniversary. Send them a card, draw them a picture, or bake something for them.
2. Remember your adopted grandparent on special holidays such as Christmas and Easter. Send them a card, draw them a picture, or bake something for them.
3. Gifts do not always have to be bought. A card is appropriate. The adopted grand-

parent would appreciate something you have made. You could even do a card on the computer. Be creative! Gifts might include: baking cookies, cake, or cupcakes, making a craft item, decorating a special picture or card, painting or coloring a picture, or putting together a special basket with small items.

4. Volunteer to help your adopted grandparent with chores. This might include raking leaves, helping them with Christmas decorations, or assisting with grocery shopping.
5. Sit with your adopted grandparent in church. You do not have to do this every Sunday. Communion is a good time to sit together.
6. Call your adopted grandparent occasionally.
7. Visit with your adopted grandparent. Invite them to your home for a meal or dessert. Take them out to eat after the worship service.
8. Invite them to special activities that you are involved in. This might include sporting events, dance recitals, music recitals, or school recognitions. You might also invite them to eat lunch with you at school.
9. When you have a school picture made, don't forget to give one to your adopted grandparent.
10. If the adopted grandparent has an illness or death in the family, be sure to visit or send a card.
11. Pray for your adopted grandparent.

Frequently Asked Questions (for use in Introductory Letters or Pamphlets)

1. Is this going to cost a lot of money?

No! It is not necessary to buy gifts. Cards are appropriate as are homemade gifts such as baked good and crafts. Our church will be planning several intergenerational events throughout the year, which are budgeted by our church. We do not charge for these events. Occasionally we might ask persons to bring a covered dish or dessert to our events.

2. Do I need to adopt all of the children in a family?

No. This is not necessary, but it is fine if you wish to do so. We have families who have separate adopted grandparents for each child or they may all have the same adopted grandparent.

3. Do I need to adopt a husband and wife together?

No. This is fine to do, but it is not necessary. Some spouses have separate adopted grandchildren and others are adopted by the same child/children.

4. What happens if I am unable to fulfill my commitment for the entire year?

We certainly understand when circumstances arise such as illness, family situations, or work constraints. We have had children and adults move during the year. When any situations arise that you are unable to continue in the program, please speak to our staff person in charge of this program or members of the Children's Committee. You are also welcome to share this with your adopted grandchild or grandparent to let them know what is happening. We will work with them to secure another adopted grandparent or grandchild if that person desires.

5. What happens when adults and children want to join the program during the year after we have already had the Adopt-a-Grandparent Recognition Sunday?

That is fine. We welcome persons to join our program at any time during the year. Please contact our staff person in charge of this program. This person will offer suggestions for people who are not adopted and contact persons to see if they would like to be involved. You will then be a part of the Adopt-a-Grandparent Program, provided information about the program, given informational sheets to fill out to give to your adopted grandparent or grandchild, and included in any events of the program.

6. I don't drive at night. Would this prevent me from being a part of the program?

Not at all! Most of our activities are planned during Sunday school or after church. There may occasionally be an evening intergenerational event to which your adopted grandchild's family may wish to give you a ride, but it is not necessary to attend every event.

7. I already have a grandchild/grandparent in the church. Should I participate?

Yes! Having grandchildren or grandparents in our church should not keep you from participating as long as your grandchildren or grandparents are agreeable. Adopted grandchildren will enjoy the relationship with your grandchildren and it is important for them to get to know many mentors in the faith community. Having an adopted grandchild gives adopted grandparents another wonderful relationship.

8. My grandchildren or my grandparents live close to me. I see them often. Should I get involved in this program?

Yes! This will give you new friends in the church family. Children need contact with many adults and adults will find that since most of our activities take place during church times, there is still plenty of time to spend with grandchildren in the community. Sometimes adopted grandparents wish to invite the adopted grandchildren to do things with their own grandchildren.

Events for Adopt-a-Grandparent Program

Many events may be planned throughout the year to bring together adopted grandparents, adopted grandchildren, and family members. The church will plan other intergenerational events, which are church-wide. Adopted grandchildren, adopted grandparents, and families are also encouraged to attend together church-wide events, but the ones listed below are planned for the participants in the Adopt-a-Grandparent Program, not the entire congregation. Remember that many older adults do not feel comfortable driving at night. For this reason, it is a good idea to plan these events during Sunday school, after worship, or in the afternoon before dark.

Adopt-a-Grandparent Recognition Reception or Luncheon

On the day that you begin your program each year, plan a special time to bring together the adopted grandparents, adopted grandchildren, and families. You might have a reception in the fellowship hall during Sunday school with refreshments. Be sure that the Sunday school classes know about this and are aware that several of their members will be absent from class. The teachers of children's Sunday school classes may wish to combine some classes. Remember that not all of your children will be involved in this program, so it is not necessary to call off your classes for the day.

Some churches provide a lunch after church. In whatever way you wish to plan your fellowship event, be sure to involve a time of dedication and prayer, if you have not already done this in your worship service. The fellowship event will be a good time to have pictures made of the adopted grandparents and grandchildren. You might also have a question and answer game in which adopted grandparents and grandchildren can interact and get to know one another.

If you have not dedicated your adopted grandparents and adopted grandchildren in the worship service, be sure and inform the congregation that this program has begun. An insert listing the participants is helpful, as is a picture board displayed in the church.

Valentine's Gathering

Have a luncheon after church that is catered or potluck. Have children make Valentines for the adopted grandparents. Another easy idea for the luncheon is to have the adopted grandchildren call his or her adopted grandparents before the luncheon to take orders for the adopted grandparents' favorite sandwiches. The children then make the sandwiches or purchase them and put together a simple sack lunch: sandwich, chips, fruit, and dessert. They can also decorate the sack. The church provides drinks.

COOK-OUT OR PICNIC

Have a cookout or picnic. Encourage the church to purchase the food if the budget allows. You might have children bring a dessert item. Do not ask the adopted grandparents to bring anything. They are the guests at this event. Play some simple games (like go fish, other card games, checkers, backgammon) or sing songs.

GAME DAY

Have children bring some of their favorite board games. Have a simple pizza lunch and let children share with the adopted grandparents some of their favorite games.

TALENT SHOW

Have the adopted grandparents and adopted grandchildren share in a Talent Show. Adopted grandparents and adopted grandchildren might do a talent together. If this is held after church, design it like a dinner theater. Serve lunch and then enjoy the talent show. You might have several families provide dishes. Let children decorate the menus. Have a selection of two-three meats and several vegetables dishes. Children might serve the adopted grandparents and then join them for the meal.

Intergenerational Events

The Children's Committee or other groups within the church may plan several intergenerational events, which may be church-wide. Some of these events may be designed primarily for children. In either case, these are wonderful opportunities for children to invite their adopted grandparents to attend with them and their family. These events will require volunteer help. Encourage your planning committee to recruit people in the church who do not have children or persons who are not involved in the Adopt-a-Grandparent Program. In doing this, your event truly becomes intergenerational. Young adults, youth, single adults, and middle aged adults are good volunteers for these events.

Traditional Advent Fair

OPENING IN SANCTUARY

Participants are asked to meet in the sanctuary, where they are divided into groups. One way to do this is to give each family, as they arrive and register for the event, a bag with an Advent symbol on it. Alternate the symbols so that you have a fairly equal division of the families into groups. You can purchase cutouts at craft and hobby stores that are ready for use. Such symbols might include: star, sheep, candle, tree, and angel. The symbol on the bag indicates which group the family will be in. As families arrive in the sanctuary, have the symbols displayed where families can sit. For example, if a family has a bag with the star on it, they are to find the section in the sanctuary where a star is displayed and sit in that section.

Ask youth or adult volunteers to dress as shepherds, and have them guide the groups throughout the evening. Each shepherd will guide one group. Have one person designated as a trumpet blower or bell ringer. If possible, borrow a *shophar*, the instrument used by the Jewish people to call them to prayer. Have one person dressed as a shepherd who will blow the trumpet or ring the bell to let the groups know when they are to go to a different room. Set up the centers in classrooms. A sample schedule is enclosed in this chapter of the book.

Families should go together during the Advent Fair. In this way, they are able to learn together about ways to share the Advent Fair in the home. They may invite special friends in the church, such as older adults or single adults to join with them as a family. If a person comes to the Advent Fair alone, they are welcomed and are placed in a group. This is an inter-generational event, so it may include singles, couples, and families with children. Youth may participate or volunteer as the shepherds or helpers in the centers.

CENTERS TO VISIT DURING THE ADVENT FAIR

Advent Wreath Room: Participants will make an Advent Wreath to be used in the home. Devotional readings will be given to each family to use with the Advent Wreath. The volunteer leader in this room will explain to the group how to put the Advent Wreath together, how each part of the Advent Wreath symbolizes, and how to use the Advent Wreath in the home.

Angel Room: Participants will make a craft that deals with angels. Volunteers, dressed as angels, will be present to tell the participants a story about the angels who told the good news of Jesus' birth to the shepherds.

Chrismon Room: Participants will make a Chrismon to be used in the home. Participants will be encouraged to include a Chrismon tree in the home. The volunteer leader in this room will explain what chrismons are and show some examples of the chrismons used in the church Chrismon tree.

Shepherd Room: Participants will decorate a shepherd cookie. They may enjoy eating the shepherd cookie as the volunteer leader of this center shares a story about the shepherds.

Four centers are usually adequate to cover the number of people in attendance; however, if you have a large congregation you might consider additional centers as well.

Jesse Tree: Participants will learn about the genealogy of Jesus. See Matthew 1:1-17. Participants will be given a small branch that can be secured in a coffee can filled with potting soil or dirt. The participants will hang symbols on the tree to represent those persons in the Old Testament who came before Jesus and who waited and longed for the coming of the Messiah. You might use the following symbols. You can find a picture of these symbols in Bible coloring books. These should already be duplicated and cut out on for persons to glue on a piece of cardstock paper or foam board. The cardstock or foam board should be hole-punched so people can hang the symbols with yarn or ornaments hangers on the branches of the tree.

Abraham	starry sky (Genesis 15:1-6)
Sarah	tent (Genesis 18:1-5)
Isaac	bundle of sticks (Genesis 22:1-19)
Rebekah	water jar (Genesis 24)
Jacob	ladder (Genesis 28:10-15)
Joseph	coat of many colors (Genesis 37:2-11)
Moses	stone tablets (Exodus 24:12-18)
Miriam	tambourine (Exodus 15:20-21)
Gideon	sword or trumpet (Judges 7)
Ruth	sheaf of grain (Ruth 2:1-15)
David	lyre (1 Samuel 16:14-22)
Jeremiah	yoke (Jeremiah 28)

Advent Calendar: Participants will make an Advent calendar. Participants will be given a pre-printed calendar that has the dates for the season of Advent. Give participants stickers that they can put on the calendar for the four Sundays of Advent. Have them write each day a word that reminds them of Advent or children may draw a symbol on the calendar. Some of the words might be: hope, peace, love, joy, and prepare. Words may be used more than one time on the calendar. Families will write down some of the words to take with them so they can write them on their calendar.

Advent Mission Project: Participants will brainstorm on some mission project they might do as a family or groups of families/friends. Have them plan ways to carry out the mission project.

Sample Schedule for Traditional Advent Fair

3:00 p.m. Registration. Receive bags with symbol on the bag indicating your group for the Advent Fair. The bag will be used to carry crafts home after the Advent Fair.

3:30 p.m. Gather in sanctuary. Explanation of events. Introduction of shepherds who will lead the groups.

GROUP ONE: STAR GROUP
4:00 – 4:20: Advent Wreath Room   5:00 – 5:20: Shepherd Room
4:20 – 4:40: Angel Room   4:40 – 5:00: Chrismon Room
5:30 – 6:00: Dinner

GROUP TWO: ANGEL GROUP
4:00 – 4:20: Angel Room   5:00 – 5:20: Advent Wreath Room
4:20 – 4:40: Chrismon Room   5:30 – 6:00: Dinner
4:40 – 5:00: Shepherd Room

GROUP THREE: CHRISMON GROUP
4:00 – 4:20: Chrismon Room   4:40 – 5:00: Advent Wreath Room
4:20 – 4:40: Shepherd Room   5:00 – 5:20: Angel Room

GROUP FOUR: SHEPHERD ROOM
4:00 – 4:20: Shepherd Room   4:40 – 5:00: Angel Room
4:20 – 4:40: Advent Wreath Room   5:00 – 5:20: Chrismon Room

Preparing for an Old Fashioned Christmas

ADVENT FAIR

This Advent Fair may be used as an alternative to the Traditional Advent Fair. Churches, who have used the traditional Advent Fair one year, may wish to alternate and use Preparing For An Old Fashioned Christmas the next year.

Preparing For An Old Fashioned Christmas does not require persons to meet in the sanctuary and be divided into groups. They can visit the learning centers as they wish. Set this up in your fellowship hall or each center in separate classrooms. Let persons spend as much time as they wish in each center, moving at their own leisure and enjoyment.

Preparation: Gather all of the supplies. Ask someone to make the Christmas stockings from felt. Have someone drill holes into the Yule Logs so the candles will fit. Order Advent candles in boxes from a supply store, catalogue, or online.

Volunteers will need to be recruited and placed in each center. Training should be given prior to the event. Provide bags for families so that they may take items home.

CRAFT AREAS

Christmas Stockings: Each family will be given a stocking to take home with them. They will decorate their stocking at the event. The stocking is to be taken home and filled with baby items that will go to community outreach center that works with families, especially families with babies. Families will be given a list of item to put it the stocking. Let families know when they are to return the stockings and offer a blessing on the stockings before they are delivered.

Yule Logs: The Yule Logs will have holes drilled for the Advent candles. Devotional booklets will be given to use with the Yule Logs. Instructions on the order to put in the Advent candles and the meaning of the evergreen, to decorate the Yule Log, should be provided.

Tree Decorations: Consult craft books or internet on many ways to decorate. Some ideas are popcorn garlands and cranberry wreaths.

Epiphany Fair

The Epiphany Fair is an intergenerational event that helps persons learn about the coming of the wise men to visit the Christ Child. Unlike the Advent Fair, persons are not divided into groups, but are able to visit the learning centers at their own leisure. Several rooms in your church will be needed or a large fellowship hall. Set up the learning centers with volunteers in each room. Some suggestions for learning centers are:

Wise Men Game Room: Have a game that teaches what the Bible tells us about the journey of the wise men. How many wise men were there? What is the color of Epiphany? What book of the Bible tells us about the story of the wise men?

Treasure Boxes: Decorate treasure boxes and fill with candy to be given to shut-ins in the church.

Luminaries: Make luminaries to remind persons of the light of the season.

Crowns: Younger children will enjoy cutting out and decorating crowns.

Spices: Display different biblical foods and spices that persons can taste and smell.

Picture with the Camel: Have a cardboard or wooden cutout of a camel. Have biblical costumes so persons can dress as wise men and take their picture with the camel.

Take Off Your Shoes: Have persons remove their shoes, which is a tradition in European countries during Epiphany. Fill the shoes with a treat.

Crayon Shavings: Make star pictures using crayon shavings. Persons use crayon shavings that are placed between wax paper and ironed, making a unique design. Instructions for this craft projects and many others may be found in craft books that are designed around the church seasons. There are many projects using the star, reminding persons of the star that guided the wise men to the Christ Child.

Epiphany Cake: Serve a traditional Epiphany cake also known as King's Cake. Recipes for these may be found in recipe books or on the Internet.

Walk Through Holy Week

The Walk Through Holy Week is an event that ideally takes place on Palm Sunday. The event is designed to help persons experience the last week of Christ life. Beginning in the sanctuary or a gathering place, participants experience a Palm Sunday processional. Travelers are then divided into groups to begin their journey through scenes in the life of Christ, which took place during Holy Week. Church members act out scenes. Each group visits the scene in the order the Bible event took place, until each group has traveled through the entire Holy Week scenes. Scenes may be revised or changed from year to year. Each scene takes about fifteen minutes to visit. While groups are waiting for their journey or after completing their journey, they are invited to the Marketplace. Potters, jugglers, beggars, weavers, bakers, and other marketplace participants help the travelers as they browse through the marketplace.

Scene One: The Money Changers

Scene Two: The Temple

Scene Three: The Last Supper

Scene Four: Garden of Gethsemane

Scene Five: The Carpenter's Shop (Jesus' cross is being made by the carpenters.)

Scene Six: The Empty Tomb

The Marketplace: Potter's Shop, Garment Shop, Juggler, Produce Shop, Spice Shop, Beggar, Bakery, Storytellers, Carpenter Shop, and Weaver

Certain scenes may be substituted for others to change the scene from year to year, such as:

Jesus at the Home of Martha and Mary

Jesus Before Pilate

Storytelling Room

Three Crosses

An old African proverb says, "It takes a village to raise a child." Those who pastor children understand that it takes a community of faith to raise a child. Children need many faith friends and mentors, who will encourage them, teach them, listen to them, and share with them. If a child is blessed to be welcomed into a church community at the time of birth and baptized in the congregation, friendships will begin very early for the child and continue into the formative years of the child's life. Sunday school teachers, Vacation Bible school leaders, Children's Church teachers, nursery workers, pastors, and many other people will become friends to the child. However, one of the most meaningful relationships may be formed through the Adopt-a-Grandparent program. By linking children with older adults in the faith community, adults share their wisdom and experience with children. Children have much to teach and share also. They will share their enthusiasm, innocence, and energy with the adopted grandparents.

Families greatly benefit from this program as well as the children and adopted grandparents. Today there are many families with children who live distances from grandparents and other family members. They appreciate the love and support of an older adult. With all of the demands on their time and energy, parents today need the support and help of the church to raise Christian children. The adopted grandparents will be an important part of this needed support and help.

The pastor to children recognizes the need for many faith friends in the lives of children, but also knows that children need older adults who will share their stories. The Adopt a Grandparent Program is one way to see that children have this link with those who have experience and wisdom. However, the pastor to children will also recognize that he or she plays a vital role in nurturing children. In the next chapters of this book, we will turn our attention to the way in which the pastor to children, or others who may be involved with children, can reach out to children. We must go out of our way to make this happen. Children need pastors and friends who will reach out to them in times of joy and crisis. This may be the senior pastor or a staff member who is the one ministering to children. This staff member, ordained or not, should view his or her role as pastor to children. Children will enjoy having the pastor visit in the home. They will appreciate him or her recognizing how important their pets are. They will especially need ministry when a pet dies. When they are ill or when family members are ill and their pastor visits, this lets children know their pastor truly cares about them, and that they are special to the church. When the children's pastor is there in times of crisis, children know someone truly understands the anxiety and fear they are feeling.

As the children's pastor celebrates with children special events, children learn that there is a friend who cares for them in times of joy as well as sorrow and pain. But how does a pastor do all of these things in ways that will be helpful and not harmful to children? The rest of the book will address these issues and offer guidelines.

CHAPTER TWO

"Mom, There's Someone at the Door!"

❖ *Visiting Children in the Home* ❖

Each year at the annual conferences held all over the United States, clergy members of The United Methodist church meet with the bishop for the clergy session. Perhaps the most significant time in this gathering is when the persons being admitted into full connection or associate membership are given the historic examination by the bishop. The bishop explains to the session that the questions he or she is about to ask of entering ministers are the same questions that have been asked of every Methodist pastor from the beginning of Methodism. These were the very questions Wesley asked his ministers. So the bishop reminds persons that they are to enter into this covenant with serious self-searching and with prayer.

Every year I wait with a sense of anticipation to hear two particular questions. It's not that I don't think the other questions are important, questions such as "Have you faith in Christ?" And there is the question, "Are you going on to perfection?" and other related questions on Christian growth. Then there are the vital questions concerning the rules and doctrines of our church. But then comes the questions I have been waiting for, number fourteen and number fifteen. These questions are: "Will you diligently instruct the children in every place?" and "Will you visit from house to house?" I want to shout, "Wait, bishop, slow down!" Let's stop and remind pastors how important these two questions are. We skip over them so quickly, and yet if taken seriously, have the power to transform the lives of children and families in the congregations these very ministers are been sent to serve.

Maybe because these two questions come side by side in the examination of candidates I got the thought indelibly imprinted on my brain that these two questions belong together. Certainly Wesley was admonishing pastors to instruct children in the church setting, but "in every place" could certainly imply the home as well. And children can be instructed in the faith by a pastor's very presence in their lives. When pastors take the time to be with children in a setting that is familiar to children, this communicates that the pastor respects and values the children. Visiting from home to home includes all ages in the church, but children are often forgotten. We visit the homebound, the elderly, prospects, the adult members of our congregation, but the children are many times ignored.

John Wesley had a great interest in the children of the Wesleyan movement. Time and again he instructed his pastors that they were to take specific measures to care for the children. Wesley also fervently believed in the importance of the home. Wesley believed the instruction and guidance of parents in faith formation were crucial for children. He taught that parents should be the primary educators of children in the matter of faith formation. However Wesley also recognized that pastors had a critical and necessary role to play in the life of children in the congregation. Not only were pastors to instruct parents in the faith, they were also to visit in the homes. They were to show interest in the welfare of the children. Wesley believed so strongly that pastors must reach out to the children in the congregation that he admonished his pastors that if they did not care for the children in their congregations, they were not fit to be Methodist pastors!

We can care for children in many ways in the congregation, but one of the best ways to show children that you care about them is to visit with them in their homes. When you enter the home of a child, you are on his or her territory. Children often see the church as the domain of the pastor, even if they feel very comfortable in their church setting. However, the home belongs to them and their family. In the home are the child's own room, his or her own possessions, his or her family pet, and it is in the home that the child can really be himself or herself. I certainly recognize the reality that many homes are not happy places. A pastor must be sensitive to this as he or she visits from home to home. Sometimes a pastor may discover insights into a child's home life where problems are evident. Counseling may be needed, or in the case of suspected child abuse, contact with the proper authorities. However, for the most part, children are glad to welcome his or her pastor to visit with them in the home. I write this chapter with the assumption that most pastors will be visiting in homes where the children are well cared for and pastors are welcome.

Pastors will want to visit children when there is a crisis, when there is sickness, or when a need arises in the life of the child. However, the visitation program that I am advocating is one that is designed for a friendly visit. The purpose of this visit is to show that you are simply interested in the child. You want to get to know the children better and to show that you care for the child's as his or her pastor. Children want to know that the significant persons in his or her life care for them. Children often look up to their pastors as role models. What better way to show children that you really care than to take the time out of your busy and hectic schedule to visit with the children? This communicates volumes to children and their families about your priority in ministry.

The visitation program can take place any time of the year, but I recommend the summer months after children are out of school. The months of June and July seem to be ideal, but if you have a large number of children you may have to schedule at certain times throughout the year. During the summer months, children are out of school and they are available during the day for a visit. This means that the pastor can schedule several visits on a designated day or days during the week and not have to visit during the evening hours. Decide which day or days you want to visit and stick with these days. Emergencies and scheduling conflict will come up from time to time in which you will have to reschedule with families, but it is much easier if you can keep to your schedule as much as possible. There will always be some families who work during the weekday and the children are not home. Some visits may have to be put on Saturday or Sunday to accommodate these families.

A pastor may have a small membership congregation and decide to visit with the children and even include the youth (teenagers). However, most often the persons visiting with the children will be the staff person who works in the area of children's ministry, be this an ordained person, laity, or in the case of some churches, Sunday school teachers. The youth pastor is also encouraged to set up a visitation program for the youth. Senior pastors in large membership congregations may consider a year-round schedule to visit with church members that includes families with children. In this case, the senior pastor will want to be sure and make an effort to include children in the visits. The priority in this chapter is to communicate to those persons who will make a one-on-one visit with children.

Several months before you plan to begin your visitation program you need to communicate with the families that you are beginning this ministry. After you set up the visitation times, you will want to send the families a letter giving the schedule. Give plenty of lead-time so that families can put this event on their calendars. Obviously some families will have conflicts due to vacation times or illness. Flexibility is a key to this program as well as the willingness of the pastor to allow for some rescheduling. However, you must also consider your time as well. You cannot spend all of your time visiting, as important as this ministry is. For this reason, make up your own visitation schedule. If a family contacts you to reschedule, try to do this. However, if you send the schedule and families do not contact you and you go by for a visit and find no one home, leave something at the door to indicate that you are sorry to have missed the child. If you want to make up this visit, that is fine, but I make it clear in my letter to parents that if I do not hear from them about rescheduling, I will come by and leave something for the child but will not call to reschedule.

Begin by gathering a list of all of the children in your church from birth to whatever grade you consider to be in the children's programming age range. Secure all of the children's addresses and place the children in groups according to zip codes or communities in which they live. I have designated my groups as "Circuits" using the Methodist concept of the Circuit Rider. After all of the children are placed in groups or circuits, a day (or days) for visitation is selected and the times are chosen. I have found it best to begin visits around 10:00 a.m., especially if you are doing your visits in the summer months. That gives the pastor time to go into the office and it gives the children time to get up and prepare for the visit. I usually plan visits for the entire day, sometimes taking a break during the lunch hours, and continuing until the late afternoon. There is a sample visitation schedule at the end of this chapter to show how times and dates might be set up.

It is helpful to find the directions of each child's home and have these in a notebook divided into sections by the circuits or locations being used. An Internet map site is very useful to secure the location of each child's home. After you have divided your notebook into sections (Circuit One, Circuit Two, etc.), place the directions for the child's home in the order you will be visiting. Be sure that you write the telephone number of the child's home on the direction page so that you can call if you get lost, get behind on your visit, or need to reschedule.

After your schedule is made up, send a schedule by mail to each family. Some families will look at the schedule and will ask to reschedule. As you get closer to the time of the visit, you will have some open dates where families have cancelled and you can rework the schedule. If you wish to send a reminder notice by mail or email, you can do this. Try to communicate with families that this visit is primarily with the children, not the parents. Obviously the parents of younger child may need to be present, but you do not want the parents to dominate the conversation or visit. When visiting a baby, a parent or caregiver will be present, but I try to hold the baby and spend some time with the infant.

Children enjoy receiving a goodie bag or gift from the visiting pastor. Always take something with you to give to the child. This does take some preparation on your part so you may wish to ask your children's committee to help you. There are several companies online or company catalogues where pastors can order inexpensive gifts such as key chains, bookmarks, books, religious novelty items, and bags of candy or suckers. If you decide to give several items, order some bags to put the items in. Before your visits, fill the bag with items appropriate for the age of the child you are visiting. Run off a label with the name of each child, fill the bag, and then place the bags in a box labeled with the circuit or location you are visiting. For example, all of the children you are visiting in Circuit One will have their bags in a box ready for your visit to that particular location. The goodie bag will have the child's name on it so that you can grab the bag when you get to the child's home. This will make it much easier when the time comes to visit. If a child is not home, you can simply leave the goodie bag at the door along with a card that says you have been to visit and are sorry you did not find the child home. When you put the goodie bag together, remember to take into account the ages of the children you are visiting. Be especially sensitive to babies and older children who are getting close to the youth age.

Take time to relax and enjoy these visits even if your schedule is hectic and may at times seemed rushed. Due to the large amount of children that I have had to visit in my churches, I have only been able to allow about a ten-minute visit in each home. However, many pastors will find they can allow between twenty and thirty minutes to visit. Don't forget to factor in the driving time needed between visits. This is why an Internet map along with directions is helpful. It will give you the driving time to each home from the church and you can obtain the driving time from one home to another.

Once you set up the visits, secured your directions to each child's home, and have the goodie bags prepared to give to the children, you are ready to begin visitation! You arrive at the first home, ring the doorbell, and are greeted by a child, who no doubt will be excited to see you. Now, what do you say? Conversations with children are very important. Of course, your very presence communicates to the child that you care about him or her, but you want to put the child at ease as you talk with one another. Here are some suggestions for visiting with children and some conversation starters.

Suggestions for Visitation with Children

When visiting children, make an effort to talk with children. Do not let parents guide or dominate the conversation. Recognize that some children are more open and talkative than others. Plan to ask questions that cannot be answered with "yes" or "no," but require the child to answer in a sentence or sentences. Some examples of conversation starters are:

"Tell me about your vacation."

"Tell me what you have been doing this summer."

"Tell me about what you like to do for fun."

"What do you like best about our church?"

"Tell me about your school and your teacher."

"Tell me about your family."

"What is the best thing that has happened to you at school?"

These conversation starters will get the child talking and you can then follow-up with questions and comments. For example, if you ask a child to tell you about his or her vacation, this can lead into a conversation about what the child enjoyed the most on the vacation. You might share about where you are going or have been on your family vacation. If the child has a pet, you could ask what the family did with the pet while they were on vacation. Did the pet stay at the vet? Did the pet go with them on vacation? A conversation might follow about the child's pet. If you have a pet, you might share about him or her.

You will feel more at ease talking with children when the conversation flows naturally from one subject to another. Do not try to force conversation. When you feel that the child is bored or tired of a particular subject, try another conversation starter. Some children are shy and quiet and you may need to use several conversation starters with them. Most of the time, however, once you get started talking you will discover that one conversation leads to another.

Take your camera with you and take a picture of the child. This will give you photographs of most of the children in your congregation. Always ask permission to take photos.

Talk to children about things that interest them. They enjoy talking about family vacations, the sporting events they participate in, their hobbies and interests, the upcoming school year, and recent church events for children such as Vacation Bible School.

Remember to use vocabulary words that children understand. At the same time, don't talk down to children.

Children may want to introduce you to their pets. If you have any anxiety about animals, let the families know before you visit. Be sure and ask the child the name of his or her pet. This can lead into a conversation about the age of the pet and how the family acquired the pet. It might also lead into a conversation about God's creation.

Most children will want to show you their rooms or their personal spaces. Some children have even taken the time to clean up their rooms. They will be ready to show you their favorite toy or toys. Show interest in the child's room and toys. Children will often want you to go outside with them to see their back yard or play equipment. They may ask you to swing them. Always be sure this is agreeable with the parents. Not all children live in subdivisions. Some children may live in apartment complexes or a downtown area where they do not have a back yard. They may want you to walk outside with them, perhaps to the nearest park. Ask the parent for permission to leave the house. If you do not feel comfortable doing this, simply tell the child that you would rather visit him or her in the home. Some children may live in rural areas, perhaps even a farm setting. If a child lives on a farm, she or he may wish to show you some of the farm animals. Ask the parent if this is agreeable and the parent may wish to go with you. If you are uncomfortable around animals, let the child know.

Some children will want you to sit down and play a game with them or play with their toys with them. If time allows you can do this, but sometimes you have to explain to the child that you have other children to visit.

Children may prepare a snack for you. Be gracious. If you can take the time to eat the snack with the child, do so. In one particular family I visited, the mom always had muffins prepared and the table set for me to join her sons for a snack. I learned to schedule additional time each year for this family as our snack time became a tradition. Some families will give you a treat and drink to take with you. This is very thoughtful and is especially helpful if you do not have time for lunch. Thank the family for their generosity.

Many times children will have a drawing for you or craft item that they have made. If possible display the artwork in your office so the child can see it the next time they are at church.

Remember to visit prospects to the church as well as church members. The visitation of prospects may be an ongoing ministry throughout the year.

If a visit runs later than the scheduled time, call the next family to let them know you are going to be late. Families have busy schedules and may need to reschedule.

If a family has forgotten your visit, don't make them feel bad about this. Go ahead and visit if this is agreeable with the family. If not, simply leave the goodie bag with the child.

If a family is not home, leave the goodie bag along with a card that tells them you have been to visit and are sorry to have missed them. Many times, families will call and tell you that they forgot you were coming. Be gracious, but unless your schedule allows, do not reschedule this visit. A sample visitation card is included in this chapter.

The first year you make up your schedule, you may not know which families work outside the home. Plan to do some visits on Saturday or Sunday if the family is not able to see you during the week. Make notes of this so that the next year you can set up a visitation schedule for all families.

Some families may ask you to meet them at a designated spot in a subdivision.

I have had several visitations around the pool. The children enjoy showing me their swimming and diving techniques. Sometimes several of my families in a subdivision have gathered at the same time. While I prefer the visits with individual families, I try to accommodate schedules and preferences.

Sample Visitation Card

REV RITA CAME BY TO VISIT!

I am sorry to have missed you at home when I came by for my summer visitation of children. I hope you have having a great summer. I hope to see you soon at church. Blessings, Rev. Rita

---

Sample Visitation Schedule

This is a sample schedule from a church in the Nashville, Tennessee area, where I served as Children's Pastor. All the names and address of families have been removed. I printed this schedule out (called "Rev. Rita's Summer Visitation), and handed it out to the congregation. Also printed on this schedule was "You will not receive a reminder notice, although we will list the circuits in the newsletter the week before the visitation."

CIRCUIT ONE: Franklin 37069

Thursday, June 3: Families one–six lived in the same subdivision, families seven–twelve lived close to the church, but not in the same subdivision.

10:00 – Family one	12:00 – Family seven
10:20 - Family two	12:20 – Family eight
10:40 – Family three	1:00 – Family nine
11:00 – Family four	1:20 – Family ten
11:20 – Family five	1:40 – Family eleven
11:40 – Family six	2:00 – Family twelve

CIRCUIT TWO: Franklin 37067

Monday, June 7: Families one–three lived in the same subdivision, families four – six lived in the same subdivision about five minutes from the previous subdivision, families seven – nine lived several miles from the two subdivisions in separate areas, but the same zip code, thus time is allowed for travel and a lunch break.

10:00 – Family one	11:40 – Family six
10:20 – Family two	1:00 – Family seven
10:40 – Family three	1:30 – Family eight
11:00 – Family four	2:00 – Family nine
11:20 – Family five	

CIRCUIT THREE: Franklin 37064

Thursday, June 10: All of the families lived in the same subdivision about twenty minutes from the church. On this particular day, I was able to finish before lunch.

10:00 – Family one	11:20 – Family five
10:20 – Family two	11:40 – Family six
10:40 – Family three	12:00 – Family seven
11:00 - Family four	

Monday, June 21: This area is a twenty minutes drive from the church and all families are in the same subdivision, allowing me to finish before lunch.

10:00 – Family one	11:00 – Family four
10:20 – Family two	11:20 – Family five
10:40 – Family three	11:40 – Family six

Thursday, June 24: Families one-three are scattered in various subdivisions off of a main road about fifteen minutes from the church. Families four–seven are in the same subdivision off of this main road. Families five and six are on the same street. Families eight and nine are in a different direction about twenty minutes from the church, but close to one another. I have allowed for a lunch break before visiting these families.

10:00 – Family one	11:40 – Family six
10:20 – Family two	12:00 – Family seven
10:40 – Family three	1:00 – Family eight
11:00 - Family four	1:20 – Family nine
11:20 – Family five	

Monday, June 28: These families are about twenty minutes from the church in various subdivisions, but close to one another. Families three–five are in the same subdivision.

10:00 – Family one	11:00 – Family four
10:20 – Family two	11:20 – Family five
10:40 – Family three	11:40 – Family six

Thursday, July 1: Families one–three are in the same subdivision. Families four–eight are in the same subdivision close about ten minutes from the previous subdivision.

10:00 – Family one	11:20 – Family five
10:20 – Family two	11:40 – Family six
10:40 – Family three	12:00 – Family seven
11:00 – Family four	12:20 – Family eight

CIRCUIT FOUR: Brentwood 37027
Thursday, July 8: These families were in different subdivisions, but close to one another and about ten minutes from the church. Due to the large number of families in this circuit, I visited into the late afternoon.

10:00 – Family one	1:20 – Family ten
10:20 – Family two	1:40 – Family eleven
10:40 – Family three	2:00 – Family twelve
11:00 – Family four	2:20 – Family thirteen
11:20 – Family five	2:40 – Family fourteen
11:40 – Family six	3:00 – Family fifteen
12:00 – Family seven	3:20 – Family sixteen
12:20 – Family eight	3:40 – Family seventeen
1:00 – Family nine	

Monday, July 19: These families were scattered throughout the city. Most were twenty minutes from the church. I have allowed for a lunch break.

10:00 – Family one	10:40 – Family three
10:20 – Family two	11:00 – Family four

Miscellaneous 37027-

1:00 – Family five	2:00 – Family seven
1:30 – Family six	2:20 – Family eight

CIRCUIT FIVE: Thompson's Station 37179 and Spring Hill 37174
Thursday, July 22: These families are thirty minutes from the church and require some driving time.

10:00 – Family one	10:40 – Family three
10:20 – Family two	11:00 – Family four

CIRCUIT SIX: Nashville and Antioch
Monday, July 26: These families require a twenty - thirty minute drive from the church. Family six lived on my same street and the parents worked during the day, thus an evening visit was needed.

1:00 – Family one	2:00 – Family four
1:20 – Family two	2:30 – Family five
1:40 – Family three	5:00 – Family six

After a few years of visitation with children in your congregation, you may wish to alter your visitation ministry. One year, you might consider having children in the same zip code or subdivision meet with you at a designated spot. You might ask children and families to meet with you at a child's favorite restaurant for lunch or to bring a picnic lunch to the closest park. The disadvantage of this visitation program is that it requires a parent to bring the children and not all of the children in the group are able to attend on the day you have selected. You might have several dates and choices for a group if you wish to try this approach. Another disadvantage is you do not get to visit one-on-one with the children. The advantage of this visitation program is that it is not as time consuming for the pastor, especially if you have a large number of children in your congregation. For some pastors, this may be the only reasonable way they can visit with the children in their congregation. This program can also be a welcome change for you and the children after you have done the home visits for several years in a row. If you decide to try this method, pastors are encouraged to visit children who have never received a visit from you in the home.

As new babies are born into the life of the congregation, it is especially important for pastors to offer support and recognition to these new children. Many churches will place a rose on the altar in honor of the new birth. Pastors will need to visit the family in the hospital at the time of birth or in the home, offering a prayer of blessing upon the family and newborn. During the Advent season, pastors can present a "Babies First Christmas" ornament to the family of the newborn who is celebrating his or her first Christmas season in the family and the church family. Some congregations choose to present this ornament in the worship service, but if not, pastors are encouraged to go to the homes of the newborn for visitation.

As the Advent season approaches, gather the names of all of the babies who have been born into your congregation during the past year. Be sure and remember to check for visitors and families who are still on your membership list, but may have moved away. Send each family a letter letting them know that you wish to visit with them during the Advent season and bring an ornament from the church. These families are then called and a time set up for the pastor to visit. The pastor takes the ornament to the family and offers a prayer of blessing on the infant. If the family has moved away from your community and you are unable to visit, mail the ornament to the family with a prayer of blessing enclosed.

"Will you visit from house to house?" If you were ordained in the United Methodist tradition, you were asked that very question. But ordained or not, if you are a pastor to children, whatever that role may look like, this question is an essential one. As pastors, we know the importance of visitation. Taking time out to visit tells persons that you really care about them. You are interested in their home life, the place where they live day in and day out. You want to get to know them in a personal way as their pastors. The home is a private domain of the family. You are not intruding in their space, but you come as one who cares about family life.

Sometimes we overlook the children in the family. We think that if we visit a family, talk to the adults, and say a brief hello to the children, that is enough. Yet children have special needs and interests. They appreciate their own special visit from their pastor. They want to be recognized as unique persons. They want to feel that they are important to you and the church. Just imagine what it means to children to have their pastor come for a visit. They will feel that you really care about them and that you want to get to know them, just them! When you enter a child's home, there will be many things to see. But among the pets, the stuffed animals, the coloring books and crayons, and the variety of toys and gadgets is the child, created by God, who yearns to be loved and respected. Will you visit the *children* from house to house?

CHAPTER THREE

"My Dog Likes to Lick!"

❖ *The Importance of Pets to Children* ❖

In one of the churches where I served as Pastor to Children and Families, the same prayer request was handed in week after week from one of our children. The child's dog was very ill, and she asked that we pray for the dog. Each week she faithfully filled out a prayer request card giving us the name of her dog. Many church staffs would have seen this request as silly, others would have ignored it, and still others might have seen it as cute. Fortunately, the staff of which I was a part took it very seriously. The request was added to our weekly staff prayer list along with persons in the church for whom we were praying. In addition, we went out of our way to let the child know that we had received her request, that we were praying for her dog, and that we understood the importance of her pet.

When the dog passed away, I immediately sent the child a card, a card that was designed for someone who had lost a pet. In addition, I contacted the child to tell her personally how sorry I was. I also told her family that I had developed a "Service of Remembrance" for a pet that I would be glad to provide for the family to use. I would come to the home of the child and share this service with the family. This service, adapted from "The Service of Blessing of the Animals" in *The United Methodist Book of Worship,* included prayers, Scripture readings, and a time to reflect on what the pet had meant to the family. The family was interested in this service and used it privately as a family to remember their pet.

Several years later this family still remembered that I had provided this ministry to them. They were very appreciative because it meant so much to the child to have a time to say goodbye to the pet to whom she was very close and the pet who was a family member.

You are perhaps wondering how in the world I would have even thought to write a "Service of Remembrance" for a pet. In another congregation where I served as the associate pastor, I received a call from an upset elderly lady in the congregation. Her beloved dog Mandy had died unexpectedly at the veterinarian's office. She was devastated at the loss of her cocker spaniel. The veterinarian had suggested that Mandy be buried on his farm, and she had called to ask if I would have a service with her and another friend. She wanted it to be quiet and reflective.

Just that year my congregation had used the materials provided in *The United Methodist Book of Worship* for "A Service of Blessing of the Animals." I remembered that she and her dog had attended this service. Since I knew of no existing services for the death of an animal, I adapted the materials to develop "A Service of Remembrance" for a pet.

We gathered on the farm where Mandy had already been buried. The service was simple and brief, but very meaningful to my friend. The only other person in attendance was a member of our church choir who sang a song about God's creation. A small wreath of flowers was placed on the grave, and we left quietly.

Ministry takes place in many ways in the life of pastors, but I learned that sometimes ministry takes place in unusual places and events that take us out of our comfort zones. I had never thought about being asked to pastor a church member in the loss of a pet, but I learned from this experience how close many people are to their pets and what a difficult loss it can be for them to have a pet die.

Like many senior adults, children are very close to their pets. The loss of a pet may be the first time a child faces death. Pets provide unconditional love, much like the love of God for each of us. As I shared conversations and visitations with children, time and again they wanted to share about their pets. Pets were important to them. Since I myself am a pet lover, I received a great deal of pleasure from having children introduce me to their pets, telling me their names and the stories of how these animals came to be a part of the family. I began to realize that a part of my ministry as a pastor of children was to recognize the importance of pets to children and to affirm this for the children of my congregation.

I began to look for biblical passages that might offer support for my understanding of the importance of animals in the life of children and families. As I encouraged the churches I served to have a "Blessing of the Animals" service, these biblical passages helped me to share with my congregation about the biblical understanding of animals. Some people in the congregation did not understand why we were having a service to bless animals. Offering these biblical passages, along with being able to share that we already had a service in place in the *United Methodist Book of Worship*, helped to gain support from some who had doubted the merits of a "Blessing of the Animals" service.

In the book of Genesis God creates all living things and declares that what has been created is indeed good.

> And God said, "Let the waters bring forth swarms of living creatures, and let birds fly above the earth across the dome of the sky." So God created the great sea monsters and every living creature that moves, of every kind, with which the waters swarm, and every winged bird of every kind. And God saw that it was good. (Genesis 1:20-21)

Not only does God create all the animals and declares the creation to be good, but God also blesses the animals.

> God blessed them, saying, "Be fruitful and multiply and fill the waters in the seas, and let birds multiply on the earth." (Genesis 1:22)

If the animals that God created are important to God, so much so that God declares all of them to be good and blesses them, we too must consider the animals we care for to be good and blessed by God.

As I looked further into the Bible I was intrigued by the story of Noah and the flood. There is an interesting passage of Scripture that is often overlooked when we talk about the story of Noah and the covenant that God made with Noah and his family. We are always glad to affirm the covenant God made with Noah and the promise that God would never destroy the earth by flood. Whenever we see a rainbow, we point to this as a sign of this covenant. What some fail to realize is that the covenant was not just made with Noah, but with the animals also.

> Then God said to Noah and to his sons with him, "As for me, I am establishing my covenant with you and your descendants after you, and with every living creature that is with you, the birds, the domestic animals, and every animal of the earth with you, as many as came out of the ark." (Genesis 9:8-10)

If God's covenant rests upon the animals as well as humanity, this means that God cares a great deal about all creation. We can bless and care for animals knowing that God first blessed them and gave them the promise of the covenant along with Noah.

God instructs humankind to take care of all creation, and Adam is given the honor of naming the animals. In biblical times bestowing a name on someone or something was an awesome task. The person bestowing the name held a certain power and authority over the one who had been named. Giving a name also meant that the person giving the name was drawn into a close relationship with the named. Even so, the animals do not offer all the companionship that Adam needs. Adam needs a partner to complete him. However, humans and animals have always been linked together. We have needed the animals for food, work, protection, and companionship.

Children like to share the name of their pets. Often an interesting story comes form children concerning the naming of pets. In blessing pets, we always use the name of the pet. When I visit with children they are always pleased when I also greet their pets and call the pets by name!

What is your pet's name?

How did you get your pet?

How did you come up with the name of your pet?

Does your pet stay inside or out?

Where does your pet sleep?

What do you do to take care of your pet?

Do you take your pet for a walk?

Does your pet like to go to the vet?

What does your family do with your pet when you are away on vacation?

(If more than one pet) How do your pets get along together?

Another way to show you care about pets is to show attention to the pets when you visit the child in the home. Let the child show you his or her pet. Call the pet by name and spend some time with the pet. If you are uncomfortable around pets or have health problems that do not permit you to interact with animals, let the family know this before you come to visit. Ask the family to show you a picture of the pet or have the child draw you a picture of the pet before you visit, which the child can then share with you when you come to the home.

If you have shown an interest in the pets of children, it is very likely that children will share with you when their pet is ill. You may even receive a request for prayer for the pet. Take this prayer request seriously. You may even want to have a prayer with the child. Talk with him or her to relieve some of the anxiety the child is feeling.

When you learn that a child's pet has died, pastors must show concern for the child and family. Immediately call or send a card to the child. I like to send a card because this is something the child can keep. I look for cards that specifically say:

"In the loss of your dog," "In the loss of your cat," or "In the loss of your pet." Have these cards ready so that when you first learn of the death of a pet you are prepared to minister to the child. Timing is important. So is action on your part. Failure to acknowledge the death of a pet communicates that children's pets are not important.

Losing a pet may be the first time a child has encountered death. Children may want to talk with you about the loss of the pet. If the pet has died unexpectedly, for example, from being run over by a car, this is difficult situation for the child to deal with. Assure the child that accidents do occur and this was not the fault of the child or the family. If the pet has died from an illness, help the child to know that the veterinarian did all he or she could to help the pet, but just as people get sick, pets also get diseases and illnesses.

Will my pet go to heaven? This is the question many children will ask their parents and you, in turn, will be asked to give your thoughts. This is always a challenging question to answer. The best answer that I have learned to provide for children is based on our understanding of God's creation. God created all animals, blessed animals, and called the creation "good." Therefore, what God has created and blessed, God will take care of. I share with children that we do not have any biblical references to what happens to pets when they die. Therefore, I cannot honestly answer the question of whether pets go to heaven. However, I can assure them that God will take care of their pets. I also tell them that the pet did not die because God needed a new pet. Children want honest answers, so be truthful. I have found that a simple, direct answer such as "I don't know if pets go to heaven, but God made your pet and God will take care of your pet," is a better answer than some long, theological answer that children cannot understand.

When a pet dies, I offer to come to the home and share in "A Service of Remembrance for a Pet." This service is given in this chapter and is based on "The Blessings of the Animals" service. The service includes Scripture readings from the book of Genesis, prayers, and a time for the family to share some memories of the pet. If a family does not wish you to come to the home for this service, make it available for the family to use.

Families in a congregation can join together each year for "The Blessing of the Animals" service. Scriptures are read from the book of Genesis. Prayers are said on behalf of the pets and the pet owners. Soothing music is sung or played on the guitar. A blessing is offered to each animal by name.

An ideal time of the year to hold "The Blessing of the Animals" service is in the fall. Many churches offer the blessing in October, close to or on the date of October 4, the Feast Day of Saint Francis of Assisi, patron saint of animals. Usually the weather is pleasant during this time of the year. Summer is too hot a time for the animals, and winter is usually too cold for the pet owners! Some churches hold the service inside, but many churches will celebrate the service in a picnic or garden area of the church, or outdoors. If you meet at the church, be sure and gain the approval of the Trustees and staff. If you decided to meet off-site, check carefully the procedures for the facility you wish to reserve. Many parks may restrict animals; however, some cities now have pet parks.

As you promote this event in your congregation, be sure that you communicate to the pet owners that each pet is to be properly restrained. Dogs must be on a leash. Cats should be in carriers as well as turtles, snakes, rabbits, and lizards. If you live in a farming community, you may even get some horses and farm animals. Welcome all of the animals, but be sure and have owners show responsibility for the care of their animals.

If you notice an aggressive dog, ask the owner to take the pet away from the blessing site. You can still bless this animal, but do so away from the other animals and pet owners. If the owner is unable to control the dog or if the dog gets in a fight with another dog, you must ask the pet and owner to leave. Give comfort to the other dog. If the dog appears agitated, suggest that the owner take the pet for a walk and return later for a blessing. If the dog is injured or too upset to stay, urge the owner to seek medical help or take the pet home. Volunteer to go to the home of either pet owner and bless the pet.

As you bless the pets, call them by name. Be gentle. Approach the animal slowly and in a calm tone of voice. If the pet is a dog, I usually try to extend my hand and let the dog smell it. Then, I gently pet the dog on the head before offering a blessing. If I am blessing a cat, most pet owners will take the pet out of his or her carrier for the blessing. I try to stroke the cat and talk softly to him or her. If you are unfamiliar with how to interact with a certain animal, ask the pet owner to advise you about the animal before the blessing.

Once the animals have been blessed, give the families a Certificate of Blessing. Don't try to have these ready to hand out the day of the blessing. It is best to have a sheet for families to sign. Ask them to print the name of their pet, what type of pet (cat, dog, turtle, rabbit, etc) and the name(s) of the pet owner(s). Mail the certificates to the owners or have them pick the certificates up at church. A sample of a Certificate of Blessing may be found at the end this chapter. A simple desktop publishing program, certificate design software or card design software will be adequate for making your unique certificate.

"The Blessing of the Animals" is an intergenerational event that all members of the congregation should be invited to participate in. Senior adults, empty nesters, and singles enjoy bringing their pets along with the children and families.

At the beginning of "The Blessing of the Animals" service, I have sometimes asked the poignant question, "Were there pets in the Bible?" While the pet owners and even the pets look doubtful, I remind those gathered that maybe it is so. Second

Samuel 12:3 gives us the story of the confrontation of the prophet Nathan with King David. Nathan speaks harshly to David after he has set Urriah, the husband of Bathsheba, in the front line of the battle, resulting in Urriah's death. Nathan tells David a story about a poor man who has only one lamb. The man has little else but this ewe lamb that he has bought. The man raised the lamb and it grew up with him and his children. The lamb shared the man's food, drank from his cup, and even slept in his arms. Sounds a lot like a pet to me!

Biblical people did not think the same way we do about animals. Animals were used for work, food, and sacrifice. We do find biblical passages that speak of the compassion of Christ using the metaphor of animals. In Matthew 23:33-37, Jesus laments over Jerusalem saying, "How often have I desired to gather your children together as a hen gathers her brood under her wings, and you were not willing!" Here Christ uses the hen, a motherly figure, to speak of his concern for Jerusalem.

With great tenderness, Jesus speaks of God's love for the lost in the Parable of the Lost Sheep. (Luke 15:1-7) The shepherd leaves the ninety-nine sheep alone to find the one that is lost! The Good Shepherd places the lost sheep on his shoulders, returning it to safety, then calls his neighbors and friends to rejoice with him. At the resurrection appearance to Peter and the disciples fishing on the sea of Tiberias (John 21), Jesus offers Peter forgiveness and reconciliation, but calls him to ministry using the image of sheep and lambs. Peter is to show the love of Christ by feeding and tending those under his care. They are like sheep who need guidance; they are like lambs who need tender care.

The prophet Isaiah has a vision of the time in which animals who are natural enemies come together in peace, with none other than a child in their midst! Who could possibly imagine this picture:

> . . . the wolf shall live with the lamb, the leopard shall lie down with the kids, the calf and the lion and fatling together, and a little child shall lead them. The cow and the bear shall graze, their young shall lie down together; and the lion shall eat straw like the ox. The nursing child shall play over the hole of the asp, and the weaned child shall put its hand on the adder's den. They will not hurt or destroy on all my holy mountain; for the earth will be full of the knowledge of the Lord as the waters cover the sea. (Isaiah 11:6-9)

Then there is the intriguing passage in Mark 1:12-13 where Jesus is driven into the wilderness and tempted by Satan. Mark tells us that Jesus was with wild beasts. What an incredible passage of the tenderness of Christ among the wild beasts as angels comes to minister to him in his time of need!

Through conversations with children, pastors soon learn about what is really important to children. Pets will inevitable come up in the conversation. As you visit with children in the home, be prepared to meet family members. Remember that some of these family members will have four paws. During the illness and death of a pet, be present as the children's pastor. The child whose pet is ill will be sad and worried. A child will grieve over the death of a pet because he or she has lost a member of the family. The child needs you as a pastor to comfort and assure them of God's goodness and love. As you care for children and their pets, know that you are following in the footsteps of One who was known as the Good Shepherd. The Good Shepherd cared for his sheep. In the same way, may you care for the children, the sheep of your flock, and the pets who mean so much to them.

Service of Remembrance for a Pet

GREETING

We have gathered here to praise God for all of creation and to witness to our faith in a God who made all of the animals. We come together in grief because we have lost a friend and a member of this family. May God grant us grace, that in our pain we may find comfort.

PRAYER

Thank you, God, for creating us and placing us here on the earth to take care of all living things. Thank you for creating the animals and giving us pets as companions. Help us to know that just as you created the animals, you love and care for them both in life and in death. Bless O Lord, the remembrance of (name of pet) and fill our hearts with thanksgiving for her/his love and devotion. Amen.

SCRIPTURE READINGS

> Genesis 1:24-25
> Genesis 2:19-20
> Psalm 65:9-3
> Psalm 104:24-26

SOME THOUGHTS ON ANIMALS

We remember that God created animals for a special purpose. When we look around our world, we see animals everywhere. They are flying in the skies, they are walking upon the earth, and they are swimming in the sea. They share in the lives of the people on this earth in a special way. God gave gifts to all living things, and this includes animals. Animals today are used to help the blind and physically challenged, to rescue individuals and to help in law enforcement efforts. Our pets love us unconditionally, just as God loves us unconditionally.

The Bible gives us many examples of the ways that God has used animals. Animals were saved from the flood and were included in the covenant God made with Noah. There are several instances in the Bible in which animals saved people. There is the story of the giant fish that saved Jonah from drowning. Ravens brought bread to Elijah when he was starving. Animals were included in the story of the repentance of the city of Nineveh. Christ came to redeem all creation and that includes the animals. A lamb is often used as a symbol for Christ.

God made us caretakers or stewards over all the creatures of the earth. We are to care for them just as we are to care for the earth and all of God's good creation.

Today we thank God for pets and the companionship they provide for humans. We remember (name of pet) as a special pet, friend, and companion.

REMEMBERING A SPECIAL FRIEND

Family members may share stories or remembrance of their pet. There may be a time of silence.

PRAYER OF COMMITAL

(*This may be used even if the pet is not physically present.*)
Care now, O God, for (name of pet), just as you care for all the creatures of the earth. Fill our hearts with thanksgiving for her/his life and help to remember him/her as a loving and faithful member of the (name) household or (name of owner). We (I) will greatly miss (name of pet).

DISMISSAL WITH BLESSING

May God who created all the animals of the earth bless you and keep you. May God strengthen us all, now and forever. Go to care for one another and for all of God's creation. Amen.

A Service of Blessing of the Animals

Adapted from The United Methodist Book of Worship

GATHERING MUSIC

(Guitar or other soft instruments may be played as persons gather and a soloist may sing soft music.)

GREETING

LITANY

Leader: God created animals for a special purpose. When we look around our world, we see animals everywhere. They are flying in the sky, they are walking on the earth, and they are swimming in the sea. They share in the lives of the people on this earth in a special way.

People: **Thank you, God, for animals.**

Leader: God gave gifts to all living things and this includes animals. Animals today are used to help the blind and physically challenged, to rescue individuals and to help in law enforcement efforts. Animals love us unconditionally as our pets and members of our families.

People: **Thank you, God, for animals.**

Leader: The Bible gives us many examples of the way animals have been used by God. Animals were saved from the flood and were included in the covenant God made with Noah. There is the story of the giant fish that saved Jonah from drowning. Ravens brought bread to Elijah when he was starving. Animals were included in the repentance of the city of Nineveh. Christ came to redeem all creation and that includes animals. A lamb is often used as a symbol for Christ.

People: **Thank you, God, for animals.**

Leader: God made us caretakers and stewards over all the creatures of the earth. We are to care for them just as we are to care for the earth and all of God's good creation.

People: **Thank you, God, for animals.**

PRAYER

SCRIPTURE READINGS

> Genesis 1:20, 24-25
> Psalm 65:9-13

SOLO

SCRIPTURE READING

> Genesis 2:19-20
> Psalm 104:24-26

BLESSING OF THE ANIMALS

God of all creation, bless (name of pet) and bless (name of pet owner) as they care for this pet.

BENEDICTION

May God, who created the animals of the earth, bless and protect you now and for-ever. Go in peace to love and care for one another, your pets, and all of God's creation. Amen.

Sample Certificate

CERTIFICATE OF BLESSING

NAME OF PET

WAS BLESSED

DATE

THE BLESSING OF THE ANIMALS SERVICE

NAME OF CHURCH

PET OWNERS: _____
PASTOR: Rev. Rita Hays

CHAPTER FOUR

"We Have a New Baby!"

❖ *Helping Children in Times of Crisis and Change* ❖

Three-year-old Sally has a new baby brother. Her family is delighted and her church family rejoices. Sally, a normal three year old and therefore egocentric in the best way, notices right away that her routine is being disrupted. Mom is away, her grandparents have come to take care of her, daddy is not home to tuck her in bed, and she missed her ballet class. There is a change in the family, and Sally is wondering if she will be loved and cared for as much as the new baby.

Ten-year-old Jack has learned that his family is moving to a new city. He has to leave behind his best friend Tommy and all of his school friends. Jack is not happy to leave his home and the security of his school routine. As he observes his family busily packing box after box, Jack is anxious that the move will mean that he will have no friends to play with and that he will not like his new school.

Nine-year-old Allison has just learned that her parents are divorcing. She is worried. Where will she live? Who will take care of her? Who will take care of daddy now that he is going to be living elsewhere? Allison is feeling guilty because she thinks she caused the divorce.

Changes and crises are difficult for all of us. They are especially challenging for children. All of us feel alone when we face an uncertainty in our life. Children especially feel lonely because they have not had the experience or years of dealing with change and crisis. So the phrase "time heals" means nothing to children. They have never been through a particular experience, so to tell them not to worry, that in a few days, weeks, or months, the hurt of a stressful event will lessen, has little impact on the child. As pastors, we must help children understand that we and other adults will be present with them. We will not let them face a crisis alone. No matter how long it takes for the crisis to ease, we will be their friend.

Children are egocentric, so when a crisis occurs they often feel guilty and blame themselves. They think they caused the disaster because they were bad or did something wrong. Pastors and family members must assure children that they are not responsible for the disaster, change, or crisis.

If, however, the child did have some responsibility, pastors and family should extend forgiveness. We have all read of tragedies in the news that involved children. A loaded gun goes off in a child's hands injuring or killing the child's sibling. While driving with her children in the car a mother is distracted by the rowdy behavior of the child and has a traffic accident that injures or kills the mother. These are especially difficult times for a child, who along with dealing with the death or injury of a family member must now share some of the responsibility. Talk with this child immediately. Let him or her know that accidents happen and assure the child that you understand he or she did not intentionally cause the accident. If the adults were partly at fault, have them shelter some of the blame. For example, in the case of the loaded gun, the child should be told that the adults were partly responsible for not following safety precautions. The child should know that the family does not love the child any less and does not blame the child in any way. Keep the child away from persons who may gossip and criticize the child. Communicate with the child's friends and adults whom the child will have contact with about discretion. The child will need continual support and affirmation from caring adults for some time.

What children may view as a crisis, adults may not. Pastors must be sensitive to the changes in a child's life that may be perceived as a crisis. Some of these events are:

- Entry into or change in school

- Birth of a new baby

- Adoption

- Death of a pet

- The family moving

- A friend moving

- Divorce

- Illness of a family member

- Child's own illness

- Loss of job by parent

- Death of a family member

- Natural disaster

All of these crises involve relationships. Children rely on relationships to help them with their own self-worth. When children are facing a break-up of these key relationships in their lives, they feel out of control. They express emotions such as anger, fear, and depression. How children interpret and work through the crisis will affect the way they are able to handle the crises they will face in adolescence and adulthood. When children work through a crisis, the process enhances their sense of self-worth, and they are better prepared to cope with future crises.[1]

Keeping secrets from children only makes matters worse. Children need to know what is happening. Pastors must be an advocate for the inclusion of children in the conversations, decisions, and family meetings during a crisis. Children are very perceptive. They have usually already figured out that something is wrong. If they are not given honest answers, they will come up with ideas of what is happening that are far from the truth. They will experience a great deal of guilt trying to decide what they did wrong to cause the crisis. Children need to be told the truth in a simple, straightforward manner.

Most of the time family members will share a crisis with the children, but sometimes pastors will be asked to intervene. Children should be told about a crisis or change in a quiet place with a trusted adult. The adult should use vocabulary that the child understands according to his or her age and developmental stage. Books are useful tools for the pastor to give to children in a crisis situation. Pastors should also gather information to give to families. There are support groups within the community to which pastors may refer families for further help and counseling.

Tell children that God and Jesus will always be with them no matter what happens. During a crisis, children will have to deal with faith issues. They may ask, "Why did God cause this suffering?" Share your beliefs according to the age level of the child. Remember that children think in concrete terms, not abstract. Pastors must assure children of God's abiding love. Remind children that when we are afraid, God is with us. God is more powerful than any crisis: death, divorce, tornado, or illness. Pastors must communicate to children that God is not the cause of bad things that happen. God created us and God created nature. God gave us and nature freedom. We can talk to children about our ability to make choices and the ability of nature to be what God created it to be. Sometimes nature brings us sunshine and beautiful weather. Depending on certain conditions, nature can bring rain, tornadoes, and storms. Assure the child that no matter what happens, God will always love him and her. The church will always care. You will be present.

God is present in the ordinary, everyday emergencies in life, so information in this chapter will deal with some of these concerns. God is also present in the very heart-wrenching tragedies of life. God's love can permeate all of life's circumstances, making the daily events of life holy moments and the tragic events of life grace-filled times. The pastor's presence and care lets children know that God is with them in all of life: the ordinary, the tragic, the good, and the bad.

Pastors should make it clear to families that they want to be available in times of crisis and change. You can communicate this to parents through the church newsletter, pastoral letters, church bulletins, and parent meetings. Let it be known that you would like parents to inform you when there is any crisis in the family. You must remind them that what children perceive as a crisis may not seem so to adults. Having one's tonsils out or tubes placed in the ears may not seem to the parent as a reason for calling the pastor. Yet these are large concerns for the child who may have never been in the hospital and is fearful of what to expect. A child falling and breaking his or her arm may not seem that great a concern to parents, but it is major to the child. Help parents understand that they are not imposing on your time when they make you aware of the concerns of their children.

One of the most frustrating parts of my ministry with children has been times in which I did not know about a child's illness or a crisis in the family. A child shows up at church wearing a cast on his arm or you find out a child has been in the hospital. You ask a child about how his dog is, only to find out he died several months ago. You learn from a member of the congregation that one of a family is expecting a new baby or a family is moving away. Keep reminding parents that you want to be informed when a crisis or change occurs. Some families will not want you to minister to them. You must respect their privacy until they are open to your ministry. Most families, however, will welcome their pastor. Children need and want the pastor to be available. In the midst of a crisis, children are often forgotten, left to suffer alone. As a pastor, you share the comforting presence of Christ with the child in crisis.

Helping Children in Times of Crisis (Guidelines for Pastors and Families)

1. Tell children about what is happening using vocabulary words children understand. Let children ask questions and give honest answers. Tell children what will happen to them.

2. Allow children to talk about their feeling and emotions. Allow children to express emotions. Never say, "Big boys (girls) don't cry."

3. As much as possible, keep the child's routine in tact.

4. Read a story with the child about the crisis. Select a book that is age appropriate. Reading stories about children who have faced difficult situations or similar crisis can be very helpful.

5. Watch a movie that is child appropriate about individuals in crisis.

6. Read Bible stories about persons who faced crisis. Share with the child about God's presence and faithfulness in the midst of the crisis.

7. Sit with the child before going to bed to offer comfort. If your child is scared, talk quietly with the child. Try to remain calm. Pray with the child. Sing a favorite song or listen to quiet music. Provide a stuffed animal.

8. Have children meet other children and families who are facing a similar crisis. Pastors can introduce the family to other families in the congregation with similar concerns.

9. Honor family traditions that may be disrupted by the crisis especially in the case of divorce or the death of a parent, or create new traditions,

10. Seek out support groups in the community.

11. Seek professional help for children if they show any signs of
    • suicide threats or attempts
    • homicidal threats
    • consequences of sexual acting out (often indicates child abuse)
    • abuse of drugs and alcohol
    • mental illness

12. Use games, puppets, and play to help children. Observe the play of children since they will use play to act out concerns or crisis situations.

New Baby

A new baby in the family is a cause for celebration, both for the family and the church. However, the birth of a sibling is often a time of stress and change for the other children in the family. This is especially true if an only child is welcoming a new addition. Children do not like change in their routine, and they often feel displaced with the arrival of a new baby. Children will notice a change in family life. They may display many kinds of feelings. They may be excited but at the same time angry or sad. A child may feel that mom does not love him as much as she once did. The child believes he or she is given less attention than before. Some children will begin to act like a baby, thinking that if they do so, they will be pampered like the new baby. Children may regress in learning skills. Eating, toileting, crying, and sleeping can be affected. The child may have temper tantrums. Some even wish that the new baby had not been born.

Pastors who understand what an older child is going through during this time can be a source of support and help to the child and the family. Your ministry will be to the baby, the parents, and to the other children in the family. Your ministry should start long before the baby arrives.

When you first learn the news that a family is expecting, contact the family. A note is appropriate, but I usually call to find out details. After offering your congratulations, you might ask the following questions:

- How is the expectant mother feeling?

- When is the baby's due date? (If the parents do not know this, ask them to call you with the due date as soon as they find out.)

- Am I able to share this news with other staff? Other members of the congregation?

- May I place your name on the prayer list? (Some congregations add expectant parents to the prayer list, giving their due date.)

- How has your child/children reacted to the news?

- What can the church do to help you? (If this is a first pregnancy the mother-to-be may need clothes or advice from other mothers.)

- Where will your baby be born? What hospital? (Don't assume it will be a hospital. Some babies are born at home.)

- Would you like some information about preparing your child/children for the birth of the baby?

After speaking with the expectant parents, I put the due date on my calendar with information on where the child will be born. That way, as the date comes closer, I can confirm with the parents when the child will be born. Sometimes doctors will induce labor or a caesarean procedure is planned, so pastors know the date of delivery. You can call the family and offer a prayer before the family goes into the hospital. Give the father your phone number to call you with the news of the baby's birth or in case of emergency.

Some pastors rush to the hospital the minute they learn that an expectant mother is in labor. I do not advise this. Expectant mothers do not want or need your presence. This is a family time and should be respected as such. If you are called in an emergency situation and the family has requested your presence, you will go immediately.

Visit the baby the day after the birth. You will want to drop by the nursery window to see if the baby is there so you can tell the parents that you saw him or her.

The baby may be in the room with the mother. Always knock on the door and ask permission to enter. Never ask to hold a baby unless the mother asks you to. Pastors should not feel obligated to hold the baby. Often when you visit, other family members will be present such as grandparents. Greet them, introduce yourself, and offer congratulations. If an older child is present, be sure and give this child lots of attention. Remind the child that he or she is now a big brother or sister. I like to take a small Bible to the parents for the new baby. I take a goodie bag or gift for the other children in the family. While visiting, I gather information for the church bulletin and newsletter such as:

- Full name of baby

- Date of Birth

- Weight at Birth

- Length at Birth

- Other Siblings

I also check to see if the family is a member of a Sunday school class or group so that meals can be provided. I ask the family if they want me to contact anyone in the church.

Before leaving, I always have a prayer of blessing on the baby even if he or she is not in the room. If the baby is in the room, place your hand gently on the baby as you say a prayer.

Be sure that the information you have gathered about the baby is passed along to the church secretary for the bulletin and newsletter. Many churches will place a rose on the altar to celebrate the birth.

Sometime during the week, contact older children in the family to offer your congratulations and to talk with them about the baby. Assure them that the parents love them very much. Talk with parents from time to time to check on the other children in the family and the new baby.

One of the greatest times of joy in the church is when a baby is baptized or dedicated, depending on your tradition. Children in the family should be included in the service and allowed to stand with the baby and parents. As the pastor to children, advocate for your inclusion in this service. You might stand next to the officiating minister and, in addition, be asked to share in the liturgy. You can present the baptismal certificate or certificate of dedication to the family. In addition, some churches present a gift.

Guidelines for Helping Children Welcome a New Baby (Pastors may share these guidelines with families.)

BEFORE THE BABY ARRIVES

1. Tell your child about the pregnancy before you tell friends. The child should hear the news from the family and not someone else.

2. If you are going to reorganize bedrooms, do this early in the pregnancy, not when the baby arrives. Celebrate with your child that he or she is now ready for a new bed or room.

3. Visit the hospital where the baby will be born. Some hospitals have classes for children.

4. Read age-appropriate books together about pregnancy and babies. Talk about what a baby does and talk about changes that may take place in the family.

5. Assure the child that you love him or her and always will.

6. Refer to the new baby as "your little brother " or "your little sister." Do not refer to the baby as "mommy's new baby" or even "the new baby." Try to use language that helps the child form a relationship with the baby.

7. Purchase a doll that is close to the size of the newborn so the child can practice caring for a baby.

8. When it is time for the birth, arrange for someone to stay with the child with whom they feel very comfortable. Try not to leave in the night for the hospital without telling the child goodbye.

AFTER THE BABY IS BORN

1. Allow the child to visit in the hospital and meet the new baby.

2. Let the child touch or hold the new baby.

3. Get others (father, grandparents, friends) to help with your older child so she or he feels special. Suggest that they take the child to his or her favorite restaurant.

4. Have a gift for the older child from the new baby.

5. Keep the older child in his or her routine as much as possible.

COMING HOME

1. Have the father carry the baby into the house so the mother can greet the older child.

2. Have the older child's favorite meal the evening you return from the hospital.

3. During the baby's nap time, spend time with the older child reading books or playing games.

4. Let the older child help with the baby such as bringing you diapers, choosing the baby's clothes, helping push the stroller, or feeding the baby.

5. Jealousy and resentment are normal emotions. Acknowledge the child's feelings.

6. Tell your child stories about when he or she was a baby and show pictures.

7. Spend some time just with your older child. Daddy might have a luncheon time or night out. Mom might have grandparents stay with the baby while you and the older child go to the park.

The Loss of a Pregnancy

Losing a child is one of the most devastating events in the life of a family. As a pastor, you must be prepared to minister to families who lose a child during pregnancy. When a miscarriage occurs, contact the family immediately to offer your condolences. Ask the family if you might provide some literature to help them. If a family has not let it be known they were expecting, they may not wish you to share this information with other church members. Always ask. If the family is agreeable, contact their Sunday school class or a group in the church to provide some meals.

Many faith traditions have prayers that can be used with a family that has experienced a miscarriage. Offer to share a prayer with the family. Many miscarriages occur in the early stages of pregnancy; therefore, families will not have named the child. However, some families will have done so. You may be called upon to offer a prayer or service of remembrance using the name of the child.

When a baby is carried to full-term or near full-term and the baby dies, families will often want to have some type of memorial service. If the child is stillborn, they may desire a funeral. Some parents want to have the baby baptized or dedicated. As a pastor, you must follow the guidelines of your own religious tradition and explain this to the parents. This is a very emotional time so you must be very pastoral.

Never tell a family that God needed a "little angel." This is bad theology. Angels are not people but messengers of God. God is loving and merciful and does not take people at God's whim. Do not tell a family that they are young and can have other children. The family is mourning the loss of *this* child. Also, do not say, "At least you have other children." Each child is unique, and no child can replace another. There are few words you can offer at a time like this. Assure the family of God's love and grace. Be honest and share with the family that none of us knows why this happened. Sometimes there are medical reasons that the medical team has shared with the family. At other times, the reasons and "whys" are a mystery. The most important part of your ministry will not be words, but your presence.

Offer ministry to the children in the family. Talk with them about their sadness. Let them know that they did not do anything wrong to cause the death of the baby.

There are now websites in which families can offer poems and thoughts about the unborn child. Pastors can mention these websites to families. Perhaps the church has such a dedicated webpage or you could encourage the church to begin one.

Adoption

I was adopted at the age of nine by a very loving family. My birth mother died when I was five and my birth father when I was seven. Since my father was ill when my mother passed away, I was sent to live at a church-related children's home. My history did not begin when I was adopted. My adoptive life was a part of my life journey. Fortunately, my adoptive parents recognized this and allowed me to share stories of my parents, my relatives, my church experiences, and friends at the Children's Home. They also gave me the strength and tools to add to my history: new friends, home, school, church, and life experiences. I did not like my middle name so I was allowed by my adoptive parents to select a new name: Melinda. My adoptive story sounds almost too good to be true. I knew who my birth parents were. I was loved and accepted by my adoptive parents. I had new friends and a supportive church. The truth was my adoptive parents fought court battles for several years before my adoption was finalized. They never gave up on me. Neither did my church.

As I relate this story, you are probably thinking of several children in your congregation who are adopted. Their stories will not be my story. Some children may not know who their birth parents were. Others may know who their birth parents are and even see the birth parents from time to time. One or more of the adoptive children may have come from a country outside of the United States and arrived at your church not speaking a word of English. Some children may be living in foster care awaiting adoption. Still others may have come out of abusive situations. Whoever these children are, and whatever their situations, you are called to minister to these children.

Children do not like to feel different. Adoptive children can often be made to feel different by other children and adults. For example, one adopted child was told that she did not have any "real" brothers because she was adopted. As a pastor to children, you can welcome adopted children in your congregation and help other children show acceptance. You can also assist families who are adopting and who want to adopt.

The adoption process requires a great deal of work for families. Enter into prayer for and offer words of encouragement to families trying to adopt. A home inspection is required, and is often a nervous time for families. Call and offer a prayer before the inspection. Write a letter of reference for families in your congregation. If the adoption process is in the court system, be willing to go and testify or be present in court, thus offering support to the family.

Once the adoption becomes final and the child has arrived, welcome the child and invite him or her to participate in the activities of the church. Introduce the child to other children, Sunday school teachers, and adults. Ask the family if you can place a rose on the altar to recognize the adoption and place information in the newsletter. Visit the family and welcome the child with a gift. You might even suggest a time in the worship service to welcome the child with a prayer of blessing.

Pastors to children can help other children and families understand that families take many different forms. You might do a Children's Sermon in which you talk about the kinds of families present in the church: single parent, parents with children, blended families, and families with adopted children. Be sure that no child makes fun of an adopted child. If you overhear this, talk with the children who are doing this and talk with the adopted child. Assure the adopted child of your love, God's unconditional love, and the love of his or her family. If there are other children in the family, be sure and talk with them about their thoughts on having an adopted child join their family circle. Help these children deal with any thoughts of jealousy and anger. You can also provide the adopted child and the other children in the family with a book on adoption.

The Bible contains powerful Scriptures about adoption. Children enjoy learning about biblical people. Children can be taught that there are several examples in the Bible of individuals who were adopted. Moses was adopted by Pharoah's daughter, who raised him as her own son. (Exodus 2:10) Esther was adopted by her uncle Mordecai, who brought her up as his own daughter. (Esther 2:7-15) Paul says that we are all adopted as God's children through our relationship with Jesus Christ. (Ephesians 1:5) Adopted children must be reminded that just as all of us are chosen and loved by God, they are chosen and loved by the adopted parents.

Adopted children experience a poignant loss of birth parents. Adoption is separation from what the child has previously known. Some children have been abused by birth parents and are re-learning how to trust adults. Thrust into an unfamiliar environment, they now deal with uncertainty and change. Some face a family that may include adopted brothers and sisters. In addition, they must make new friends, go to a new school, and sometimes learn a new language and culture. No wonder many of these children express, anger, grief, and confusion. Families may be dealing with adopted children who have physical and mental challenges. Go out of your way to offer pastoral care to these families. Pastors can link adopted families with other families in the church who have adopted children. You can also suggest support groups and professional counseling to deal with problems.

As the pastor to adopted children and families, your role is to offer unconditional love. After all, everyone is a child of God, and everyone is adopted by a loving God who will never forsake us.

Guidelines for Helping Adopted Children (Pastors may share these guidelines with families.)

1. Be accepting of whatever feelings the adopted child has. These feelings can range from love to sadness, anger, jealousy, grief, and fear.
2. Realize that it takes time for adopted children to feel a part of the family and the church. Be patient with the bonding process.
3. Be sure the child's teachers, school, church, Sunday school teachers and other adults are aware of the adoption and any problems the child is having.
4. Discuss positive use of adoption language. Birth mother (father) or birthday mother (father) may be used. Do not use "real" to refer to birth parents.
5. Whatever name the child uses for the adopted parents, use that name when talking with the child about the parents.
6. Respect the child's ethnic background. Plan some events and celebrations that recognize the child's cultural background.
7. Having a naming ceremony or welcoming ceremony in the home or church.
8. Create a photo album or scrapbook for the child giving information about birth parents, other siblings, former foster parents, or other family members.
9. Cooperate with the birth parents during a child's visit or gain the cooperation of the birth grandparent or relative. Adopted parents will need to determine safety issues and emotional issues when a child visits birth parents.
10. If there are birth children in the home, recognize that it will take time for them to accept the adopted child. Prepare these children ahead of time, but realize they too may have feelings of jealousy and anger.
11. Provide books for the adopted child and other children in the family.
12. Have a neighborhood "get acquainted" party for the adopted children and neighborhood children.
13. Help children and adults understand that families are formed in many ways.
14. Help children and adults understand that children are adopted for many different reasons and adoptions may occur at different ages.

Recommended Books on Adoption

Annetta Dellinger, *Adopted and Loved Forever*, Concordia Publishing House, 1987 (For children ages 4-7)

Sherrie Eldridge, *Twenty Things Adopted Kids Wish Their Adoptive Parents Knew*, Dell Publishing, 1999

Keiko Kasza, *A Mother for Choco*, Penguin Putnam, 1992

Lois Ruskai Melina, *Raising Adopted Children: Practical, Reassuring Advice for Every Adoptive Parent*, HarperCollins, 1998

Sofia Stergianis and Rita McDowall, *What Is Adoption?*, Wisdom Press, 2006

Moving

Most adults do not consider moving a crisis. While we are sad to leave behind friends and a familiar place, often we are moving due to a new job or to upsize or downsize our living space. If we have to move due to a divorce, this is certainly a time of crisis for adults as well as children. In most cases, however, adults embrace the move as a necessity. We accept the fact that we will make new friends and find a new community of worship. Children perceive a move as a separation from the familiar. This is especially true if the move is out of town and away from friends. The child wonders if he or she will find new friends. They worry about the new school. Moving can be a time of crisis and upheaval for children. The security they once felt in their home, the place where they feel protected and safe, disappears.

Pastors must be sensitive to new children who move into your community and come to visit the church. Greet any visitors and be sure and find out if they are new to the community. Give them information about the church, but also connect them immediately with other families in the church. Contact them by phone or a note giving them additional information about your family and children's events. If your church has a Wednesday night dinner, invite them to come and be the guests of the church. Be sure there is a family on hand to greet them and sit with them at dinner.

Show the new family where the Sunday school classes are and introduce them to Sunday school teachers. Welcome them to attend the activities of the church family.

Some churches have a business directory that lists the businesses and hobbies of church members. This is helpful for new people who have moved in the community and are visiting the church. Many times, they do not know whom to call upon for work at the home or personal needs. The business directory provides the names of persons in the church who can be trusted as honest, caring businesspersons or persons with hobbies and trades.

When a family moves away from your community and leaves the congregation, say goodbye to the family, especially the children. Acknowledge the family during worship, in the newsletter, or during a church event. Write them a letter expressing your appreciation and care for the family. If you are aware of churches in the community to which they are moving, give the family this information.

The Bible teaches us that we are to extend hospitality. The people of Israel went out of their way to welcome the stranger and traveler, because they knew what it was like to be without a home. At one time, the nation of Israel had been a wandering people without a place to call home. So they cared for the outcast, the less fortunate, and the stranger in their midst. Christian believers also practiced hospitality. They ate with one another, shared their possessions, and cared for the widows and the poor. They welcomed people of all different backgrounds and places to join their community of faith. As a pastor of children, you can model this biblical mandate to be hospitable. Welcome the strangers who move into your community and visit your church. When you do this, especially when you welcome the children, you will be teaching that God is a God of hospitality. God is a God who welcomes us, not as strangers, but as children of God.

Divorce

Divorce represents a loss for everyone in the family. For children, this may be the first major crisis of their lives. The family is the center of a child's world. Now the family is divided. Children not only grieve, they yearn for security in the midst of change and upheaval. When a child learns that his or her parents are divorcing, they sense that a change is about to occur in their life and the family's. The parents may show anger and resentment toward one another. Parents may use children as a way to fight each other. They may place the child in a most uncomfortable situation, using the child to carry messages to the other parent. In addition to parental conflicts, there may also be economic hardship, changes, and a child's loss of contact with a parent who has been an authority figure. The child wonders if he or she will have to move, go to a new school, or which parent she or he will live with. A child wants to know what will happen to the other siblings in the family. Will the siblings live together or will they be separated by the divorce? Many children experience psychological, social, and academic problems. The child has a great deal of questions and a great deal of pain.[2]

The following are questions pastor need to be aware that the children may ask:

- Where will I live? Will it be in the same house or do I have to move?

- Who is going to take care of me?

- Will I be left alone?

- How can I keep mommy and daddy together?

- Will I get to see dad or mom?

- What is going to happen if I get sick?

- Who will take care of my meals?

- Where will daddy or mommy live?

- Who will take care of mommy or daddy?

- What will happen to my brothers and sisters?

- Will I get to keep my pet?[3]

Each child is unique and we cannot predict how individual children will cope with divorce. However we do know what child experts tell us will probably happen at certain ages. Before the age of three, children do not have the cognitive development to understand what separation means. It is best to give a very simple explanation to this age child such as, "Mama and daddy are going to live in different houses." This explanation must be continually repeated as a young child learns through repetition. The child needs a primary home that is very stable and secure. They should have brief, but frequent visits with the parent with whom they are not living. Visitation confirms that both parents love them and care about their needs. [4]

Younger children (age three to five) must have concrete answers for the reasons for the divorce. These children think in concrete, logical terms. These egocentric children will want to know how the divorce is going to affect their lives. The children need assurance that the divorce was not his or her fault. You might say to the child, "Daddy and mommy have been fighting a lot so we have decided in live in separate houses." The older child (six to eight) has the cognitive ability to understand more information than the preschooler. Most will understand the word "divorce." They probably know of other children whose parents are divorced. These children will fear being abandoned. These older children have fierce loyalty to both parents. Communicate to them that both parents love them equally. School-age children (nine to twelve years old) come with a strong moral sense of right and wrong. They are rigid in their beliefs. Immediately they will want to know who is to blame, and they will probably pick sides. Expect this, but share with the child your love. Do not play one parent against the other. Be honest at all times.[5]

Children may experience many symptoms of anxiety and stress during the divorce process. Some of the physical symptoms may be restlessness, loss of appetite, increase in pulse rate, diarrhea, frequency in urinaration, sleep difficulties, trembling, and bad dreams. Some children will deny that the divorce is happening, or they may remain silent, saying little. Some children may regress to thumb sucking or bed-wetting. Many children will blame themselves for the divorce. Others will have fantasies that the parents will reconcile. Children find themselves in a stage of panic and confusion, because their world has been turned upside down. The ways parents interact with children during this time are vitally important. Some children may need professional help to deal with this crisis.[6]

Churches must work to redefine family so congregations recognize that all types of families exist in the church. As the pastor to children, you can help your congregation understand that there are many forms of family. You can also plan events that include all persons. When an event is planned that requires a parent to be present and a divorced child's parent cannot be present, arrange for a friend in the church to step in. Take into account that the children of divorce may not be able to be present every Sunday for worship and Sunday school. Help teachers to understand this and encourage them to provide materials for children who are absent. If you have ministries in which children take part, such as acolyting and choirs, be sure that the children whose parents are divorced get included. Ask parents to give you the dates of which Sundays these children will be at church. They can then be scheduled on these Sundays to participate in serving the church.

When you learn a family is going through a divorce, contact the family to offer support. Provide books and materials for the family. Talk with the children. Let them know they are not to blame for the divorce. Tell them that both parents love them. Help families maintain a routine in the home and outside the home. Link the family with church members who might help. Transportation might be provided to church or other activities the child is involved in. Remember that many families will have less money to spend, so you might help these families with the cost of church activities.

If a parent decides to remarry, the church should welcome the new spouse or children in the family. Advise a divorced parent to wait sufficient time before dating. If you have any reservations about a future spouse, be honest, for the sake of the children.

Remind the parents that even though they are no longer husband and wife, they will always be father and mother to their children. Remind them also that, due to the children, their relationship with their ex-spouse will continue beyond the divorce, so the divorced parents will need to find constructive ways to communicate and connect in order to support their children. The most important thing you can do as a pastor to children experiencing divorce is to support and love them.

Guidelines for Helping Children of Divorce (Pastors may share these guidelines with families.)

1. Let children know that both parents love them.
2. Do not force your children to choose one parent over the others. Do not put pressure on them to take sides.

3. Do not argue in front of your children.
4. Assure the children of financial support. If you are the parent required to pay child support, honor this with regular and timely payments.
5. Do not ask the child which parent he or she loves more.
6. Do not criticize your ex-spouse in front of your children.
7. Allow the child to have a relationship with the ex-spouse's family.
8. Don't ask the child to keep secrets from the ex-spouse.
9. Don't compare your child to ex-spouse in a negative manner. Example: "You are lazy just like your father."
10. Keep a routine in schedule and keep changes to a minimum.
11. Work together with your ex-spouse in co-parenting.
12. Develop a visitation plan and a plan for holidays.
13. Keep family traditions and rituals or recreate new ones.
14. Don't date immediately after a divorce.
15. Keep your child informed of dating relationships. If you decide to remarry tell the child the details. Do not let it come as a complete shock to the child.

Recommended Books on Divorce

YOUNG CHILDREN

Lawrence Brown and March Brown, *Dinosaurs Divorce: A Guide for Changing Families*, Little and Brown Company, 1988

Linda W. Girard, *At Daddy's on Saturdays*, Albert Whitman and Company, 1987

Vicki Lansky , *It's Not Your Fault, Koko Bear*, Book Peddlers, 1998

Fred Rogers, *Let's Talk About It: Divorce*, Putnam's Sons, 1966

OLDER CHILDREN

Maxine A. Ford, S. Ford, and J. B. Ford, *My Parents are Divorced, Too*, Magination Press, 1997

Linda C. Johnson, *Everything you Need to Know About Your Parent's Divorce*, Rosen, 1992

Jill Krementz, *How it Feels When Parents Divorce*, Knopf, 1998

BOOKS FOR PARENTS:

Melinda Blau, *Families Apart: Ten Keys to Successful Co-parenting*, Perigee, 1995

Robert E. Emery, *The Truth About Children and Divorce: Dealing with the Emotions So You and Your Children Can Thrive*, Penguin, 2004

Vicki Lansky, *Divorce Book for Parents: Helping Your Children Cope with Divorce and its Overmath*, Book Peddlers, 1996

Nicholas Long and Rex Forehand, *Making Divorce Easier on Your Child: 50 Effective Ways to Help Children Adjust*, Contemporary Books, 2002

Wallerstein, Judith and Sandra Blakeslee, *What About the Kids?: Raising Your Children Before, During, and After Divorce*, Hyperion, 2003

Child Abuse

Children who are abused learn a powerful life lesson: the world is an unsafe place in which to live. Can you even comprehend the fear these children live with day in and day out? Children love their parents and other adults who care for them. Yet to these children, love means pain. Similar to children facing other crisis, abused children will have feeling of guilt for events of which they had no control. A part of this guilt is to wonder what the child did that was so bad. They begin to reason that they must have indeed done something very bad to be treated so abusively. Some abusers will tell the child that it is his or her fault. Thus, abused children are left with pain, hurt, and a hopeless situation. These children have no way to protect themselves. If they ask for help, they are fearful that the family unit might be shattered. To keep the family intact, they must tolerate the abuse.[7]

What do these abused children do to survive? One child will withdraw and become shy and quiet. Another might be very active, always moving to get out of the way of the abuse. A third might try to please his or her parents, striving to do everything right, and become like a parent to the abusive parent. A fourth may be angry and show aggressive behavior by striking out at others. All of these children are simply trying to survive in the cruel world they inhabit.[8]

The pastor to children is called to help abused children, but we rarely learn about the abusive situation. These children do a good job of hiding their pain. They do not often ask for help. If, however, you learn of any abuse, you are mandated to report it. Someone tells you about the abuse, or you may observe behavior or marks that are suspicious. Most states have Child Protective Services and you should immediately contact them. Do not attempt your own investigation. Leave this in the hands of professionals. You can put yourself in danger if you go to the home to investigate reports of child abuse. Certainly it is difficult to turn in a member of your congregation. You may fear that the abuse is not founded or that the parents will be upset with you. In this situation, you must work on behalf of the child. You are not obligated to find proof. You are required to report and let the authorities handle the situation, even if you encounter the hostility of a family.

Churches should always have a Child Abuse Prevention Policy in place. An excellent resource for formulating this policy is *Safe Sanctuaries: Reducing the Risk of Child Abuse in the Church*, authored by Joy Thornburg Melton. Your policy, which should be formulated and approved by the church leaders, states exactly what to do in the situation where you suspect child abuse. Some states are now requiring that the person who observed the abuse must report. Some church's child abuse policies instruct teachers, childcare workers, and others to report to the senior pastor or associate pastor who would then report the abuse to Social Services. Be certain what your state law is. If you already have a Child Abuse Prevention Policy in place, have an attorney look it over to be sure you are in compliance with current laws. Regardless of what your state's policy is on reporting procedures, you will need your teachers, childcare workers, and Scout leaders to inform you of any allegations. Be sure that all groups who use your church have a copy of your Child Abuse Prevention Policy. This includes all of your Sunday school teachers, childcare workers, workers with children at special events, Boy and Girl Scout leaders, and other community groups that use the church when children are present. My advice is to always have two workers with children at all times. This is for the safety of both the children and the workers.

As pastor to these children, it is very important that you help the child disclose his or her secret. The first way to do this is to report to Child Protective Services and let them investigate. If a child has been abused, he or she will probably be removed from the home. If the allegations are not founded, the parents may leave your church. Be aware that this may happen. As best you can, talk with the family and explain why you or another person had to report. I would rather have a family leave the church than risk the safety of a child. If possible, suggest professional help for the parents.

If the abuse has been experienced, and you are able to see the child, give the child the opportunity to talk and share as he or she wishes. Do not force a child to talk or to give details of the abuse when the child does not want to share. Reassure the child that the abuse was not his or her fault. The child did nothing wrong. Be supportive of the child because the abused child will have low self-esteem. Talk with the child about God's love and faithfulness. Abusive children will often extend their loss of trust in persons to a lack of trust in God. Children will wonder how God could support the parent's behavior and still be a God who is loving and protective. Children may be fearful or angry at this kind of God who they perceive has punished them through the abusive parent. You will have a lot of bad theology to help the child overcome. Children must learn to trust again. Talk of God's love and trust. Be available, as you can, to offer love and support.

What about the abuse of children that is nonfamilial? Again, children are very reluctant to report this abuse. They may have been threatened by the perpetrator or told that harm will come to the family. Usually the child will report the abuse only after direct questioning by someone who may have noticed a change in the child. As a pastor, be aware when you notice major changes in a child's behavior and attitude. Some of these changes are:

- Withdrawing and not communicating

- Making sexual advances to other children

- Nightmares and trouble sleeping

- Problems eating or with bowel functions

Do not assume that one or more of these symptoms necessarily means a child is being abused, but do consider abuse as a possibility, especially if there is more than one of the abovementioned presenting at the same time.

All members of the victim's family need the support and care of the congregation. You can provide materials, suggest support groups, and encourage professional counseling. Let the family know the child will need professional help immediately. Always let the child know that you believe his or her story. Assure the child it was not his or her fault in any way. Affirm the child's willingness to tell and express sorrow at what happened to the child. Offer the child protection and support from his or her pastor. Express to the parents that you are confident in their ability to care for the child. The parents will have overwhelming feelings of guilt. Be nonjudgmental. Agree to go with the family to court if there is a hearing or trial. Your presence and support will speak volumes to a family undergoing the horror of child abuse.

Recommended Books on Child Abuse Prevention

Bill Anderson, *When Child Abuse Comes to Church: Recognizing Its Occurrence and What to Do About It*, Bethany House Publishing, 1992

Lory Freeman, *It's My Body*, Parenting Press, 1984 (Preschool Age Children)

Linda Walvoord Girard, *My Body is Private*, Albert Whitman & Co., 1992 (Ages 4-8)

———, *Who is a Stranger and What Should I Do?*, Albert Whitman & Co., 1993 (Ages 4-8)

Chris Hansen, *To Catch a Predator: Protecting Your Kids from Online Enemies Already in Your Home*, Dutton Adult, 2007

Sandy Kleven, *The Right to Touch: A Read-Aloud Story to Help Prevent Child Sexual Abuse*, Illunimation Arts Publishing Co., 1998 (Preschool Children)

Joy Thornburg Melton, *Safe Sanctuaries: Reducing the Risk of Child Abuse in the Church*, Discipleship Resources, 1998

Dave Pelzer, *A Child Called It: One Child's Courage to Survive*, Health Communications, Inc., 1995

Cornelia Maude Spelman, *Your Body Belongs to You*, Albert Whitman & Co., 2000 (Preschool – Grade 2)

Addiction

When an individual lives an addictive lifestyle—whether alcohol abuse, drug abuse, sexual addiction, or eating addiction—it is very easy for persons outside of the family situation to be judgmental. Due to misinformation or lack of information about the nature of these addictions, even church people have been critical. They have found fault with the addicts and criticized the family. Families have been too embarrassed to share with the church and their pastor because they felt they would be judged. Family members have been led to believe that they are partly to blame because they could not control the family member. Out of love and concern, they have enabled the addict, and the family is left to deal with much guilt. Many addicts have been told continuously that they are failures. They have been told that "if they would just try harder" they could overcome their addictions.

As a pastor to families dealing with addiction, you need to get correct information about the causes. Addictions are often biological. Addicts have a disease, just like any person dealing with a life-threatening illness. There is no cure for addiction. Persons may be in recovery, but they are never cured. They will be addicts until the day they die. Most addicts relapse after a period of recovery. Those who stay clean and sober recognize the power of the disease and know they must work on their recovery daily. Living one day at a time is the only way addicts can stay in recovery and not relapse. The road to recovery is a long and difficult journey. Many addicts face an addiction that is coupled with a mental illness. Some addicts are dealing with a dual diagnosis such as drug addiction along with an eating disorder. Addiction is a family disease affecting every member of the family. If there are children in the family, they will be affected by the disease of the parent or sibling.

Read all you can about addiction and mental illness. Be able to communicate to church members about these diseases and clear up miscommunication. Attend some Alcohol Anonymous meetings or meetings of Narcotics Anonymous. You can find a list of meeting times and places in your community on the internet. The list will indicate whether the meetings are open or closed. An open meeting means that anyone may attend. A closed meetings is for addicts only. Being in the room with addicts and hearing their stories will help you as a pastor to understand the struggles these persons are facing. You also need to learn about the community support groups, detoxification centers, and rehabilitation centers in your community and state. Keep books and materials on addiction available for families and church members. You may have families come to you asking your advice on where they can go for help.

If a family comes to you about an addiction, never be judgmental. Always offer support and prayer. Confidentiality is a given. Advise them to go to a detoxification center or rehabilitation center if they are unable to stop their addiction without professional help. Very few addicts are able to stop their addictions without some type of professional help. The Twelve-Step program is used by almost all rehabilitation centers. Some of these centers are outpatient based so that a person may work and attend sessions. If a person is staying in your community, connect them immediately with a local Alcohol Anonymous group, Narcotic Anonymous group, eating disorder group, or dual diagnosis support group. All of these groups will practice the Twelve Step program and will connect the addict with a sponsor. A sponsor is an individual in recovery who will work with the addict in completing the twelve steps of the program. The sponsor also offers support and understanding, because he or she has faced many of the same challenges. Pastors and family members can offer support, but they can never understand what the addict is going through. Only a fellow addict has the ability to relate to another addict's story.

When there are children in the family, the pastor must be especially sensitive to their needs. Children must never be told they are to blame for a parent's addiction. They should be encouraged to attend support groups for children. You can provide them books and reading materials on addiction. Be sure that families communicate with children about addictions that are biological. Tell children that the parent or sibling who has an addiction loves them, but the person is ill. Let children know that the parent or sibling may have to leave for a time to get help. Never should a woman stay in an abusive situation with an addict. For the safety of the children and her own safety, advise a mother to go to a center for abused women.

Pastors can be advocates for allowing recovery groups to meet in the church. Workshops dealing with addictions can be offered. Do whatever you can to clear up misinformation and provide adequate information on addictions. Create an atmosphere where families dealing with addictions feel welcomed and supported by the congregation. Your understanding, love, and support will be a vital ingredient in the recovery process for addicts and their families.

Support Groups for Families

Families Anonymous: www.familiesanonymous.org

Al-Anon/Alateen: (Al-anon is for spouses of alcohols and Alateen is for children of alcoholics) www.al-anonalateen.org

Codependents Anonymous: www.codependents.org

The Hazelden Foundation: www.hazelden.org

National Alliance for the Mentally Ill (NAMI): (800) 950-6264

Tragedy in the News: Natural Disaster, Violence, And School Shootings

April 16, 1998 is a date that many will not forget in the quiet town of Bowling Green, Kentucky. A major hailstorm and flood hit the city with a fury, knocking down power lines, destroying over 4,000 cars, damaging thousands of homes, and causing millions of dollars in property loss. I was serving in the community as an associate pastor at a large downtown church. Although the destruction was citywide, the worst damage occurred in one neighborhood where many of my church members lived. After it was safe to get out in the neighborhood, I parked my car and walked to the home where I had church members. I went to minister to the families and the children, offering them comfort and support. Some of the children were frightened. This tragedy had hit home; it was in our community, not some place far away. Thankfully, no lives were lost, but the children were filled with anxiety, fear, and stress. What I could offer was a caring presence and giving them the assurance that they would be safe. I also sent out a pastoral letter giving guidelines to parents when children experience a tragedy.

News reports are filled every day with stories of violence in the world. There are senseless stories of murder, natural disasters, terrorist bombings, and school shootings. Children see violence depicted in shows, movies, and video games. Children are affected by the terrible acts of violence they witness and hear about. Helping children deal with tragic events is important for the pastor to children. How the child will cope with a tragedy will depend on his or her age and individuality. A child who is already fearful and anxious may have a harder time than other children. Also, a child who has dealt with a recent loss, such as a death in the family, a divorce, or other trauma will likely have more problems dealing with the tragedy.

Families will often turn to the church in times of tragedy. We witnessed this in the United States after the 9/11 terrorist events. Churches were filled with worshipers, and pastors were asked to offer comfort in the midst of tragedy. Many people turned to their pastors for answers about why there was so much suffering. Pastors to children should be available during these times of tragedy to talk with children and answer questions. Children need to know that the church is a safe haven and place of refuge.

Children of all ages will come into contact with violence and tragedy. Insulating the young child from tragic events best helps younger children, especially toddlers and preschool age children. Turn off the television or restrict the child from viewing channels with news coverage. Many pictures shown on television are too violent for young children. Young children have a hard time telling the difference between fantasy and reality. The young child may not understand that the "news" is real. Older children should not watch news coverage of a disaster by themselves. Adults should watch with the child and talk about the events. Older children should only watch a limited amount of television. If a child has questions, answer these. Children need the security of knowing that they can talk about fear and worries. Older children may have lots of questions and want to talk about why something happened. When talking with children, you might find out what they already know about the event. These will help you better discuss about the event and know how much information to provide. Follow the child's cues to see how much she or he wants to talk. If the child does not seem to want to talk, just offer a simple explanation of the tragedy and ask if he or she has any questions. After a child has time to think and reflect, she or he may come up with other questions. Provide facts that are age appropriate. Don't ever tell a child simply not to worry or to forget about the tragedy. Encourage children to talk about any fears or feelings.

If the child has in some way been involved in the tragedy, assure the child she or he is safe now. Let them know that they did not cause the tragedy to happen. Children who have witnessed tragedy often need to talk about it. Experts tell us this will not further traumatize the child, but will help him or her. Children may also want to draw or playact about the event. A stuffed animal is usually a comforting gift for a younger (and many older) child who has faced a tragic event. After a tragedy occurs, it is helpful to the child to continue his or her regular routine. Be sure the child feels that he has a safe, supportive, and loving home and church environment.

Professional help may be needed if the child is having problems. Some symptoms of post-traumatic stress are fear, anxiety, physical problems such as headaches and stomach pains, bedwetting, nightmares, behavioral problems, fighting, loss of appetite, and sleeplessness.

Churches and families could encourage children to help victims and families of tragedy. Most religious groups have relief agencies already in place so that money can be send to them. Children might give some of their allowance to these agencies or collect donation items through the children's program at the church. They can also say prayers for the victims and light a candle.

Children and families will turn to pastors for advice on dealing with tragedy. They may question God and be angry with God. Help them to understand that God knows our hurt, our pain, and our fear. God is always with us even when we feel alone. Children need to know that God watches over them and is with them at all times and in all situations, even the tragedies of life. Here are some Scriptures to share with children:

Psalm 23:4

Psalm 27:1

Psalm 46

Psalm 91:11-13, 15

Matthew 10:29-31

John 14:27

John 16:33

Romans 8:35-39

Philippians 4:7

Guidelines for Helping Children Deal with Violence (Pastors may share these guidelines with families.)

1. Watch to see how often your child uses the internet and watches television. Monitor your child's use and teach your child safety measures for internet use.
2. Be sure your family practices gun safety if you choose to have a gun in the home.
3. Unload and lock up all firearms.
4. Be sure the church has a Child Abuse Prevention policy as well as safety policies in the event of fire or natural disaster.
5. Watch for signs that children are displaying violent behavior: cruelty to animals, being drawn to violence, using physical violence, exhibiting poor school performance, showing signs of substance abuse, or committing any criminal activity or disrespect for the property of others.
6. Read books together on peace. Recommended books are listed in this chapter.
7. Use healthy ways for children to express feelings such as play dough, painting, puzzles, toys, puppets, stuffed animals, music, stories, and play.
8. Take a look at the child's school to see that safety measures are in effect and enforced.
9. Determine the safety of your children when they are on the school bus. If you ever observe drivers talking on cell phones or speeding, report this to the school board.
10. Provide opportunities for children to reach out to other families who have faced tragedies.
11. Teach children to show respect for law enforcement, paramedics, fire fighters, and other rescue workers. Churches might hold an appreciation dinner or lunch. Invite one of these persons to share with the children after a tragedy has occurred.

Recommended Books on Peace-Making

Joan Walsh Anglund, *Peace is a Circle of Love*, Gulliver Books, 1993 (Ages 4-8)

Jane Baskwill, *If Peace Is . . .*, Mondo Publishing, 2003 (Ages 4-8)

Jeremy Gilley, *Peace One Day*, Putnam Juvenile, 2005 (Grade 3-6)

Edie Julik, *Sailing Through the Storm: To the Ocean of Peace*, Galde Press, Inc., 2000 (Ages 4-8)

Todd Parr, *The Peace Book*, Little, Brown Young Readers, 2004 (Kindergarten-Grade 2)

Vladimir Radunsky, *What Does Peace Feel Like?*, Atheneum/Anne Schwartz Books, 2003 (Kindergarten-Grade 2)

Sandy Eisenberg Sasso, *Cain & Abel: Finding the Fruits of Peace*, Jewish Light Publishing, 2002 (Kindergarten–Grade 3)

Katherine Scholes, *Peace Begins With You*, Little, Brown Younger Readers, 1994 (Ages 9-12)

Jane Breskin Zalben, *Paths to Peace: People Who Changed the World*, Dutton Juvenile, 2006 (Grades 4-8)

The Ministry of Presence in Times of Crisis

I lived for several years in the state of Kentucky. Persons often remarked that if you did not like the weather, just wait; it was likely to change in a moment. Life is like that for children and families. One moment life is filled with routine, security, and safety. Families go about their everyday tasks. Then a crisis occurs, and family life is turned upside down. This crisis can be a divorce, a move, a new addition to the family, death, illness, violence, or a natural disaster. In the midst of these crises of life, families need to know that the church cares. Pastors are present to offer compassion, help, support, and love.

We enjoy the times of celebration with families: at the birth of babies, at the baptism of children, at graduations, birthday, anniversaries, and times of recognition and honor for family members. Yet, it is your presence in the time of crisis that means the most to families. They probably will not remember much of what you say, but they will remember that you were there and God was there. With your very presence, you bring the presence of Christ, the one who was well acquainted with suffering and pain. Through you, the love of Christ will be evident. And through Christ, no crisis will be unbearable. The situation is painful, sad, tragic, but not hopeless. Carry the hope of Christ to families in crisis and let them know that no circumstance, not even death, can keep them from the love and grace of God.

Chapter Four Endnotes

1. Andrew Lester, *Pastoral Care With Children in Crisis* (Louisville: Westminster John Knox Press, 1985), 48-59.

2. Robert E. Emery, *The Truth About Children and Divorce* (New York: Penguin Group, 2006), 61.

3. Ibid., 29.

4. Ibid., 112-113

5. Ibid., 113-119.

6. Ibid., 73-74.

7. Andrew D. Lester, editor, *When Children Suffer* (Philadelphia: The Westminster Press, 1987), 128.

8. Ibid., 129.

CHAPTER FIVE

"Someone I Love Died."

❖ Helping Children Deal with Death ❖

W hen my mother passed away, my older son was a teenager and a part of the youth group at the church where I served as associate pastor. When the youth group learned that Allen had lost his grandmother they immediately sent him a sympathy card. The youth director contacted him to express her sympathy. When we returned to church after the funeral, many of the youth surrounded Allen with their presence and let him know that they had been thinking of him. His youth group was very supportive in the loss of his grandmother.

My son Ben had the opposite experience. Ben was a child at the time his grandmother died and did not have the youth group to offer condolences. He did not receive any cards, phone calls, or expressions of sympathy. Yet he had Sunday school teachers, friends, and pastors in the church.

As a pastor of the church, I received many words of sympathy, love, and concern. Flowers were sent to the funeral home, many cards arrived at our home, and persons brought food. Being caught up in the middle of my own grief, I did not realize how affected my sons were by the concern or lack of concern from the congregation in the death of my mother and my sons' grandmother. Years later, when we were reflecting on her death, my older son shared that he had appreciated the outpouring of kindness from his youth group. My younger son, however, painted a different picture. He had felt rejected, alone, and forgotten by his church during this time. As Ben shared about his experience of being ignored, there was a note of bitterness in his voice. I could tell he resented that, as a child, his grief seemed unimportant to his congregation.

Like adults and youth, children grieve. Of course, their ability to understand death and what it means will depend upon the age of the child and the individuality of each child. When a death occurs, family members are often so consumed with their own grief that they do not think about what children are going through. They may not be able to offer children the support they need. Families are often confronted with many decisions: deathbed goodbyes, funeral and burial arrangements, taking care of the loved one's belongings, and other difficult choices. During these times, children are often ignored, and they are seldom included in the decision-making process.

As the pastor to children, you must be aware of the needs and concerns of the grieving child. You can be an advocate for children during this difficult time. You must be present to offer support to the children, but you can also encourage parents to include children in some of the decisions. Children who are prepared can make the decision whether to visit a dying loved one, attend a funeral or visit the cemetery. Death is a crucial time for the grieving child and adults should remember to include children in the decisions and recognize the grief that children feel. Children are often what I call neglected mourners, forgotten by the very people that they love and respect. If we value children as an important part of our congregations, we must not forget them when a death occurs. Instead, we must reach out to them with compassion.

The first step you can take as a pastor of children is to begin to understand the grief process that children may go through. What this process will look like will depend upon children's ages and their developmental stages. We must also recognize that each child is an individual. Even with our understanding of the grief process and the developmental stages, not all children will follow these in a precise manner. Each child will grieve in his or her own way. We need to be aware of the children with whom we work, their unique personalities and abilities, and be patient with them as they grieve. We must also have a listening ear and an understanding of the individuality of children. We also need to read books that give us a better understanding of the grief process and the developmental stages of children.

As a pastor to children and families, you can communicate your understanding of this grief process to parents. Often you can share this with the families before a loved one passes away, especially if you have a situation where a family member is dealing with a terminal illness. This gives the family time to grasp an understanding of what children are going through and will prepare them to help the child when a death occurs. You are also prepared as a children's pastor to offer support and understanding based on the age and developmental level of the child. A brief summary of the reaction of children at different age levels will help you begin to think about children and their reactions to death.

Even before a person close to the child dies, children are already aware of death. They see dead birds and insects as they play in the yard. They observe dead animals lying on the road that have been hit and killed by drivers. They may see death several times a day on the television. They may have had a pet die. If they have read any fairy tales, they have encountered death. Children will often act out death in their play roles. Death is a part of life, and children are aware of it.

As pastors to children we should not be surprised to find the children of our congregation reacting in different ways to death. Children respond to death in different ways depending on the individual child. Some children will ask lots of questions about death. Others may seem unconcerned about the death of a grandparent but will show great emotion at the death of a pet. Some children may never talk about death, but as they play they will act out dying. One child may ask lots of questions. Another may say little, but may be willing to draw a picture about the death of a loved one. Some children may want to read a book about death and talk about it, while others will just listen to the book being read and say very little. Some children may initially react to the death by crying or asking questions, but soon may start playing. All of these reactions are normal as each child is an individual. Let each child grieve in his or her own way, but be present to offer love and support.[1]

Children age two and under will sense that something is different in the family routine. The atmosphere in the home may be tense and filled with more activity as persons come in and out of the home to visit and express condolences. Family members whom the child, does not know or has not seen before, may come to stay, creating a different environment and a different routine than the child is used to. At this age the child will not understand what death is but will know that something is different in the daily routine. The young child may become fussy, cling to parents and siblings, and even show some aggressive behavior.[2]

A parent may express this concern to you. Assure the parent that this is normal because the child's routine has been altered. Encourage the parents to assume a normal routine as soon as possible since this age child needs structure and reassurance. For example, perhaps the child is used to a bedtime story or a time of rocking and cuddling before bed. The parent may have stopped doing this in his or her own grief and the business of taking care of so many details during the death process. Encourage the parent to assume the routine that gave the child comfort and a sense of well-being.

Let the parents know that the child two years and under will not remember the person that has died. It is important for the family to have pictures and to share stories with the child as he or she gets older.

The child three years to five years will think of death as temporary. That is, he or she will believe that the person who has died will return. Sometimes the child will substitute the attachment they had for the deceased person to another person. This is normal and should not upset the family. It is also normal for the preschool child to feel sadness for a short time but then escape into play. The family may think that the child is not grieving, but the child can cope with the loss by assuming a normal routine, and play is a good way to do this. Like the child two year and under, this age child may not remember the person who has died, so pictures and memory sharing by family members will be important as the child grows.[3]

It is possible that this age child (three to five) may have nightmares and aggressive behavior. He or she may not want to follow rules or be disciplined. The child needs a daily routine and structure in his or her life, which has often been disrupted at the death of a family member. As a pastor to these children you must show the child lots of affection and reassure him or her of your love and concern. Encourage family members to do the same and to resume normal activities as soon as possible. If the child is close to a relative such as a grandparent, aunt, uncle, or cousin, the child might wish to spend time with this relative who can offer comfort and attention which the immediate family may not be able to provide.

The preschool child thinks very concretely, not in abstract terms. During the preschool years, children think in magical terms so they may believe that the loved one will return. Since the preschool child is very egocentric, they may view themselves as the cause of bad or good things that happen. Therefore, when you talk with children about death at this age, keep your comments in very simple terms. Children will realize that persons to whom they are close to are very sad at this time. Death may not be personal to them except that it has upset the routine in their life and the life of their family. As a pastor to children you might discuss the sadness that we feel when someone dies, but express the assurance that God made us and will take care of us when we die.

Some young children will ask questions immediately, others will be silent at the time, but come back later with questions. Answer each question with a simple answer. Children learn through repetition. They may ask the same questions over and over again and need you to give them the same answers. You might approach conversations with a young child by speaking about the absence of functions that are familiar to the child. For example, when a person dies you can tell the child that the person will no longer breathe, eat, talk, think, or feel any more. When the child's dog's dies, we might share with the child that the dog will never bark or run again. These are experiences that the child can relate to and will help the child to understand that the person or dog is not returning.[4]

As you talk with preschool children, do not equate death with "sleep." This is confusing and will give the preschool child the impression that the person is returning You might use the example of death as a part of the life cycle. Children are familiar with nature and the life cycle. They will be familiar with leaves falling from the tree each year and plants dying in the garden. It is extremely important to reassure children of this age that they are not responsible for accidents, deaths, or injuries. Being very self-centered as this age, they will often believe they are at fault. As a pastor to children, you need to tell them time and again that they did not do anything to cause the illness or death of a loved one. This is a part of life. Accidents and illnesses happen. Let them know that God did not cause the death of a loved one. God loves us, but people get sick and people have accidents. When we die, God continue to love us and take care of us. Let the child know that the family members will be sad and the child may be sad. This is normal when someone dies.

Telling children that sickness is the cause of death can cause children anxiety and worry. Preschoolers cannot discriminate between a serious illness and a minor one. Let these children know that a serious illness may cause death. We all get sick sometimes, but we usually get better again. This will alleviate some of the anxiety that these children may feel if they get sick or a family member is ill.

We must also be careful when talking with the preschool child about older people dying. We may relate to the child that as a person get older, it is natural for them to have more illnesses and eventually die. However, when a young person dies, due to an illness, the child is confused. It is probably best to share with children that most people live a long time before they die, but some don't.

Around the age of six to nine years, a child will begin to understand that death is final and permanent. This age child may begin to have a fear of death, afraid of his or her own death and the fear of others dying, especially family members. They may also blame themselves for the death and feel great guilt. Children may begin to ask specific questions about death. Since this age child is often worried about someone close to them dying, they may begin to be compulsive in caring for family members or clinging to family members. They may not want to be left alone with baby sitters. Some of these children will have headaches, stomach problems, and phobias.[5]

Encourage these children to seek out safe, familiar adults who are able to discuss some of their deep-seated fears and concerns. As the pastor to the children, answer questions honestly, but assure them that they are loved and will be cared for by the family and church. You might ask them to draw a picture of how they are feeling or of an activity they enjoyed sharing with the deceased person. Talk about this picture with the child. Let the parents know that the physical symptoms will disappear, but the family should take them seriously and give the child lots of love and reassurance that the child is not responsible for the death. If headaches, stomachaches, and phobias continue, family members should be encouraged to seek medical help.

Grade school children need physical, tangible ways to experience and express grief. Rituals such as visitations, funerals, and memorial services are very important. Children of this age will accept the religious beliefs of parents and the church. A belief in life after death generally comforts children as they deal with the death.

As children near the age of abstract thinking, age ten to twelve, they will begin to understand that death is inevitable and irreversible. They will still retain some feelings and thinking that they are guilty or responsible for death. They will begin to ask questions about the body and the funeral. They will also ask religious questions about God and what happens after death. Like the younger children, these children may also display physical symptoms of headaches, stomach pains, and phobias. They may also have trouble with schoolwork and the inability to focus on play or other tasks.[6]

For most children, the physical symptoms and difficulties with schoolwork should improve as time passes. During this difficult time it is vitally important for the child to be affirmed and cared for by the family, the pastor to children, and the church. If it continues, encourage the family to seek professional help.

As the pastor to children who are in the middle and older elementary ages, answer questions about illness, death, hospital, and operations in an honest and open manner. These older children will discover that some people are responsible for their own deaths, while others are not. Be willing to talk with them about this. Children of this age will be aware of good and evil. Reassure them that God is at work in the world even when there is evil present.

Children will not use the same logic as adults. Children often use magical thinking when it comes to death. That is, they believe that a momentary thought, wish or action actually caused someone's death. For instance, a child may accidentally break a dish while visiting his grandmother. The grandmother may say, "Child, you'll be the death of me yet." If, a short time later the grandmother dies of a sudden illness, the grandchild may think, "If I had been good and not broken that dish, my grandmother would still be alive." Or a child may be jealous of her baby sister and wish she had not been born. Later, if the sister dies of Sudden Infant Death Syndrome, the child may believe she killed her baby sister. If a parent in the family dies, the child may remember a time in which he or she used harsh words with the parent or had a temper tantrum. Now the child may think that due to his words or his behavior, the parent has died. A child may feel so guilty about a death that he or she cannot even talk with an adult about what his or her feelings are.[7]

You can see why it is important for the pastor of children to have a good relationship with the children of the church and be present when they face a death. Children will often talk with the pastor when they would not talk with a family member. You can assure the children that they did absolutely nothing to cause the death.

Some children may feel guilty because they were not able to use some imagined power to help the deceased person. They might say, "If I had only beaten that cancer up my father would not have died." Assure these children that there was nothing they could have done to prevent the death. Other children may think some external forces caused the death. The child may not understand that a life threatening illness caused a sibling's death. They may tell you that it was caused by a demon, witch, a ghost or some other imaginary creature. Children's pastors and parents should help the child understand what really caused the death.

Adults will often grieve intensely, but children have the ability to grieve intermittently. Adults are often puzzled when they see children crying at a funeral service, but running and playing later in the day. There will be times of on-again, off-again grief that may lead adults to believe that child have recovered from his or her grief. This is not true, however. Persons who work with children believe that children have periods of grief and of non-grief as a means of self-protection. Actually children's times of grief are not any shorter than adults and sometimes longer.[8]

Like adults, certain circumstances and events may re-trigger grief in children. A child may have experienced grief at an early age, but as she or he gets older situations may occur that remind the child of the death of the loved one. The child may readdress the grief they experienced as a young child. For example a child who loses his father at the age of five may be more aware of his death at the age of eleven when he has a Boy Scout camping trip and his father is not present. Feelings of grief for his father may resurface at this time.

As the pastor to children, be aware of the children in the congregation who have lost parents. Be sure the child has an adult friend to be with them on occasions when you plan events that require a parent or grandparent to attend. For example, if the church plans a Mother-Daughter Banquet, be especially sensitive to the child whose mother has died. This child should not be excluded from the banquet. Arrange to have a lady in the church invite the child to the banquet. The same goes for other events the church may plan that require children and parents or grandparents.

Holidays are difficult times for families who have lost loved one. Pastors may forget that grief does not recognize the ecclesial timetable of the church. The church seasons of Easter and Christmas are times of celebration and anticipation for the Church. Yet persons dealing with grief are in the season of Lent. While the Church is rejoicing in the good news of Easter or anticipating the glad birth of Christ, grieving worshipers are filled with sorrow and sadness. Reach out to families at this time. Offer them hope in the midst of their grief. Remind them God is faithful in each season of our lives. Give them some devotional materials or books to read to help with the grief process. Share with the family some Bible verses on suffering. You could mention the passage of Scripture where Jesus weeps over Jerusalem (Luke 19:41-42) or Jesus weeps at the death of his close friend Lazarus. (John 11:1-44) There are the beautiful and assuring words of hope in the Gospel of John, chapter 14. You could offer the Easter story as a passage of hope.

Pastors must show compassion and understanding when families do not wish to attend services or events during the holidays. Many churches are recognizing that the holidays can be depressing for some people. A service of worship may be planned during the shortest day of the year called "Service of The Longest Night," which occurs during the month of December. Quiet music is played, candles are lit, Scriptures of hope and peace are read, and there is a time to reflect. You can find ideas for this service on the internet, and several denominations have resources available.

Pastors can suggest to families that they remember the loved one during holidays or church seasons. They could carry on a family holiday tradition in memory of the loved one. You might suggest the family plan to plant a flower in the spring or place flowers in the church on the anniversary of a death as a way of remembering the deceased. Write down the date of the death of the loved one so you can send a note or make a phone call on the anniversary of the death.

When you first learn of a death that affects a child in your congregation, let the child know that you are available to listen and talk. Speak to the parents and ask how you can help. The parents may not yet know how to answer. Remind them that you are available and make sure they have your phone number. Acknowledge the child's loss and grief. Immediately contact the child's Sunday school teacher, choir leaders, and other friends in the church and ask these persons to extend sympathy to the child. Encourage the child's peers in the Sunday school class and other groups in the church to send a class sympathy card or make cards for the child. When the congregation is informed of the death through the bulletins, newsletters, or worship services, make sure that the children are included in the announcement and not just the parents. This lets the children know that you are aware of their grief and that children are important to the congregation in this time of loss as well as the adults.

Pastor should express condolences to the child personally. Visit the child in the home or send a card depending on whether this was a close family member or a distant relative. Make sure the parents are agreeable to your visit. For example, I had one situation where a child's grandparent passed away, but the family did not wish me to visit, feeling that the child would be more traumatized by being bombarded with visits. I had to respect the wishes of the family. Provide a book on death that is theologically sound and age appropriate for the child. A list of some recommended age-appropriate books are listed at the end of the chapter. Be available to talk with the child. Keep in contact with family members and observe the child at church.

Parents may contact you to ask if it is advisable for a child to attend the funeral or memorial service. This is certainly the decision of any family, but you can give them information based on the developmental abilities of children to understanding death at certain ages. Given what we know about preschool children, they will probably not understand what is happening. However, elementary children may be able to remember many parts of the service. Some funeral homes have coloring books that help the children to understand what is going to take place at the funeral. If not, make sure the parents go over with the child what is going to happen at the funeral and the cemetery, explaining to the child in vocabulary words he or she can understand. Or you may be the one to explain the funeral to the child. The child needs to be prepared for the experience. You will find guidelines at the end of this chapter to help you and the parents prepare the child for the visitation in the hospital or sickbed, the visitation at death, and the funeral.

If the family feels that the child is too young to attend the funeral and the service is being held at the church, arrange for childcare. Children may be encouraged to attend the funeral or memorial service and make visits to the cemetery, but never force them. They are members of the family and have a right to take part in such events, depending on their age. Attending will often clear up the fantasies and fears they have. Visiting the grave periodically may initiate a discussion of how and what they are feeling.

Parents sometimes become worried that their child may need professional help to cope with death. Any kind of extreme behavior can be a signal that the child may need professional counseling. Such behavior could be suicide threats; destructive acts toward property, people, or animals; frequent panic attacks; or substance abuse. Other "red flags" might be the inability or unwillingness to socialize or a continued decline in school performance. Books are excellent tools to help children talk about death and deal with their feelings. In this chapter, some signs are discussed that pastors of children and parents should look for that will be present in children as they grieve. These signs do not necessarily mean that the children need professional help. They are the normal ways children grieve.

Your presence as the pastor to children is more important than a lot of talk that means little to the child. Too much information and answers to questions that children haven't even asked can confuse children. At the time of death, it is more important for you to be supportive and loving as the children's pastor and to answer questions honestly. Always keep in mind the age and developmental level of the child. Gather materials that you can give parents about children and death. Most important, let the children know that you care and the congregation cares. Your congregation is the child's church family and to ignore a child at the time of death is to communicate to the child that he or she is not really a valued member of the community of faith. In this chapter, there are some guidelines for sharing with children about death and being present with children at the time of death. There are also some suggestions for ideas to share with parents to help children at the time of death.

Be there with grieving children in their time of need. You come as Christ's representative, extending the message of God's grace and comfort. Such a ministry of presence conveys meaningful witness to the love of God for those who grieve.

Guidelines for Helping Children Deal with Death (Pastors may share these guidelines with families.)

1. Make immediate contact with the child. If the child has lost a close family member, make a personal visit. Make sure the parents are agreeable to your visit.
2. If the family member was not close to the child—for example, a distant aunt that the child did not know very well—send a card.
3. Find a good book to give to the child. It should be theologically sound and age appropriate.
4. Give the parents information that will help them in understanding the grief process of children at certain ages. Also give them guidelines on children attending the visitation and funeral. This information should be offered. Be aware that some families will not wish to have the information. Respect the wishes of the family.
5. Keep in mind the developmental stage and age of the child to whom you are talking. Talk with the child openly and honestly. Answer questions truthfully. Don't give children more information than they need.
6. Volunteer to be present with the child during the visitation, especially the first time the child views the body of the deceased.
7. Pray with the child.
8. Be sure that your newsletter, bulletin, and other announcements of the church include the name of the child in the family as well as the adults.
9. Contact the child's Sunday school teacher and other important adults in the congregation in the child's life and encourage them to extend condolences to the child. Ask the child's Sunday school class, choir, or other groups the child is a part of to send a card or make cards for the child.
10. If the service is being held at the church, provide childcare for children whose parents do not wish them to attend the service.
11. Ask the child to draw a picture, write a poem, or remember the loved one in some other tangible way.
12. Observe the child when you see them at church. Talk with the parents from time to time to make sure the child is going through the normal grieving process and problems have not surfaced that may need professional help.
13. Be aware of church functions that the child may feel uncomfortable attending.

Arrange for the child to have an adult in the church attend with them, for example at a Mother-Daughter Banquet or Father-Son Campout.

14. Be careful of the vocabulary words you use with children. Do share your faith. When sharing faith with children, use simple vocabulary. Theological ideas are often abstract and confusing. Use concrete, practical terms. It is more important at this time that you are present and loving than that you offer some great theological truth that the child may not understand and that may only confuse him or her.

15. Avoid making God the cause of death. For example, many well-meaning people will say to a child, "God loved your mother so much God took her to heaven to be with Him." The child will reason that since God also loves him or her and his other family members, perhaps God will take them also. Also avoid saying, "God needed another angel, so God took your grandmother." Angels are not humans but special messengers of God. This may lead children to resent God.

16. Affirm the child and give them love and encouragement as you see them at church.

17. Be prepared ahead of time. Have books already ordered that are theologically sound and age appropriate. Also have materials ready that you can share with families.

Some Signs of Mourning in Children

Guilt: Children will often feel guilt when a loved one dies. This is especially true for younger children. Children need someone to talk with about these guilty feelings, and they need to be assured that they did not cause the death.

Anxiety and Stress: Children will exhibit fear and lose a sense of security. Young children may cling to parents, and become very demanding. They will not want to be separate from the parents.

Sleep Difficulty: If you talk with a child about death using the terms, "the person is asleep," this may cause the child to fear death. The child will be afraid to go to sleep thinking that he or she will also die. Dreams and nightmares may be common in children.

Sadness and Crying: The sadness and crying among children will vary from child to child. Some children will cry and others will not. Some children will remain sad for a long time and others will not. Some children will hide their sadness. Carrying an object that was meaningful to the deceased may help children.

Anger: Children may become angry with God or adults. If they feel responsible for the death they will become angry with themselves.

Physical Complaints: Some of the more common complaints of children who have experienced death are headaches, stomachaches, and inability to sleep.

School Problems: Children may have difficulties in concentrating, remembering, and other difficulties with schoolwork and social interaction with school friends.[9]

What Parents Can Do

1. Assure the child that you love him or her.
2. Explain the death to them, keeping in mind the developmental level of the child. Someone close to the child should tell the child about the death. Choose a quiet location to talk with your child where you will not be disturbed. State the facts, as you know them. Allow the child to ask questions and answer them to the best of your ability. Wait quietly with the child, as he or she may need time to react to what you are telling them.
3. Avoid certain phrases when talking with children about death. These include:
   • "He or she is asleep." (Children will think the person is coming back and they could fear going to sleep at night.)
   • "The person has gone on a long journey." (Children will think the person will eventually return and will keep looking for them.)
   • "The person has passed away or expired." (These are vague terms and young children do not understand them. It is best to use the word "died.")
   • "Now you will have to be the man of the house." (The child is not a substitute adult and we do not want to deprive children of their childhood.)
   • "You remind me so much of your brother." (Each child is unique and is not a substitute for a dead sibling.)
   • "God took your mother because she was such a good person and God needed her in heaven." (This causes the child to resent God.)
4. Do share with the child that the person who has died loved the child, the person was not angry with the child, and the child did not in any way cause the death. Also communicate with the child that the person is not returning.
5. Your physical presence is important during this time. Staying close to the child will reassure them. This will also give you the opportunity to observe your child and learn his or her reaction. Some children will wants hugs from you or to sit close to you. Bedtime will be an important time to cuddle. Be sure and let your child know that they are loved and safe.
6. Avoid making God the cause of death. For example, many well-meaning people will say to a child, "God loved your mother so much God took him to heaven to be with him." The child will reason that since God also loves him or her and his other

family members, perhaps God will take them also. Also avoid saying, "God needed another angel, so God took your grandmother." Angels are not humans but special messengers of God. This may lead children to resent God.

7. Be careful of the vocabulary words you use with children. Do share your faith. When sharing faith with children, use simple vocabulary. Theological ideas are often abstract and confusing. Use concrete, practical terms. It is more important at this time that you are present and loving than that you offer some great theological truth that the child may not understand and may only confuse him or her.

8. As much as possible, maintain a normal routine. This is often challenging when a death occurs. However it is important for children to have a normal routine for dinner, homework, chores, and bedtime. You need to also realize that your child may have a difficult time concentrating on schoolwork or falling asleep at night. So be flexible when children are having problems with school work or sleep.

9. Help your child to maintain good physical health. Death is a stressful time for families and children. Make sure you child gets enough sleep, exercise, and nutrition.

10. Pray during this time as a family. Have your child draw a picture to help express his or her feelings or write a poem.

11. Being with friends and teachers can often help the child regain a sense of normalcy. Invite friends to come over and play with your child. Be sure and talk with teachers about the death so they are aware of what is going on and can be observant to see signs that indicate your child is having problems coping with the death. Some children will show difficulties with school after a death. A grieving child may have difficulty concentrating, sitting still, or doing challenging assignments. Talk to the child's teacher and school staff so they can be aware of any changes in the child's normal behavior.

12. Gain support from your pastors and congregation.

13. If you decide the child is going to the visitation and funeral, talk with them beforehand. Explain to them what they will be seeing and what will happen at the funeral. Do not force children to attend.

Helping Children Attend the Visitation and the Funeral

Talk with the child about what is going to happen. Give specific details. Tell the child what the room will look like where the body will be viewed. Tell what the casket looks like. Let children know that the body will look different from what the child may remember. The skin will look paler and the body will be cold because it is not working anymore. Talk about how adults at the funeral or visitation may act. Let the child know that there will be crying and laughing. Many persons may tell stories about the life of the person who has died. Help the child understand that this is normal.

Only have the child approach the casket if they wish to do so. No child should be forced to view the body unless they desire to do so. Viewing the body may help some children understand what death is and that the person is indeed dead. You will want to let the child view the body the first time in private with a supportive adult. Invite the child's pastor to be present. The child's age and stage of development is critical when trying to discern whether to have the child view the deceased.

School age children may wish to help the family with some of the decisions about the service. They might choose a song, write a poem, or help select the burial clothes.

Help children find ways to express their feelings. They might write a letter, draw a picture, or place something in the casket. They might make a photo album. The family might choose to display photographs of the loved one at the service or visitation. The family might also choose to plant a tree or make a charitable donation in the deceased's memory. Families can also later visit the grave with children. These times should be to remember the person. Make sure children know that this is not a magical time to contact the deceased. If the family chooses to say words when they visit the grave, assure the child this is a means of comfort to the family.

Since the parent of a child may have lost a spouse, child, or parent, he or she will be mourning, and may not be able to provide the child with the needed support. Other adults such as friends, family members, and pastors will need to comfort, answer questions, and care for the child during the visitation or service.

If the service is being held at a church, arrive early so the child can speak with the pastors.

When Children Visit the Dying

1. Many hospitals do not allow children under the age of twelve to visit. This is changing, however, as hospital staffs realize that such visits can be of value to the child and the person who is dying. A child should be given permission to visit someone who is important to him or her if this is agreeable to the hospital patient.
2. Prepare the child for the visit. Help him or her to know what will be seen and heard. The child will need a description of what the patient will look like and what equipment may be in the room.
3. Introduce the child to the nurses and other medical staff who are caring for the loved one.
4. Help the child to understand that he or she is not to touch equipment in the patient's room, including the television set.

5. Make the visit short. Children are active, and after a while will tire of the visit. The patient also needs rest and does not need a lengthy visit.

6. If visits cannot be arranged, the child can telephone the patient. Hearing a child's voice can help make a dying person know he or she is loved and cared for. Be sure both the child and the patient agree to the telephone call.

7. Children can also make cards for the patient or bring flowers or balloons if permitted by the hospital.

8. Never force a child to visit. Never make a child feel guilty because she or he does not wish to visit.

9. Visit the nursery of the hospital so children can see that the hospital can be a place of joy and birth, even in the midst of death.

10. Have a prayer with the loved one before you leave. Let the child offer a prayer if she or he desires.

Suicide

In one of the churches in which I served, I had the tragic experience of dealing of two suicides in which children lost loved ones. Death is an emotional and sad experience for children, but it is especially difficult when the death is caused by suicide or another traumatic experience. Children, like adults, are very confused.

In one of the situations, the grieving child was in grade school. The parents were able to explain to the child that her brother had killed himself. They even shared with the child how this occurred and that the brother had been very depressed for a long period of time. They assured the child that it was in no way her fault. This close-knit family knew that they had to be honest with their daughter. She had been very close to her brother. The parents conveyed to the girl how much her brother loved her.

Sharing this kind of news was very difficult for these parents. They sat down with the child in a quiet place at home. They gave the facts, but did not give morbid details that were not needed. They allowed the child to cry, offering her hugs. They remained with the child and assured him that they would be present for the child. In the days ahead they tried to keep the child's routine as normal as possible.

In the other situation, the child was much younger. The family did not choose to tell the child at the time what had happened to his grandfather. They did tell him several days later after they had time to grieve and talk with the child. Initially they told the child that his grandfather had an accident and he died. When pressured for more information in the days ahead, they sat down quietly with their son and explained what had happened.

It is difficult to know what to do when a suicide occurs. Families wonder how much to tell a child. As the pastor to children you may be asked to step in and talk with the child. One thing is for certain; you need to be immediately present with the child and the family to offer support. If you have been asked to share with the child, find a quiet place so you can talk in private. If the parent wishes to be with you, agree beforehand what and how much you will say to the child. In most situations, the parents will share with the child about the suicide and you will be there to offer support and pastoral care for the child. However, you can share some guidelines with the family if they request.

How much information to share depends on the age of the child and how the child may react to the initial news. If the child is kindergarten age and younger, you can say to the child, "Your brother had an accident. He died because of the accident." That may be enough information at the time to satisfy the young child. However, if the child presses you for more information, it may mean he or she is ready to accept more. If you as the pastor are the one to share the child the news of the suicide, be sure that the parents wants you to share more. You may need to say to the child, "Your parent will talk with you more later."

When this traumatic news is shared with children, there are various reactions. Some children will yell, cry, and scream. This is difficult to watch, but the child needs to release his or her feelings of shock and sorrow. This is the experience I witnessed with the child whose brother had committed suicide. She was crying passionately and could not be consoled. I had the opposite experience with the child who lost his grandfather. He was sullen and silent. At times he tried to run away and hide. Neither of these two reactions is unusual. Again, as with adults, the reaction will depend upon the child.

Consider the emotional maturity of the child when sharing information about suicide. Children, however, are more resilient than we think. The child needs trusted adults who will share in a loving, caring manner. I would rather provide age appropriate, truthful responses, especially when a child continues to insist on knowing more, than to make up stories that will have to be changed later. When a child, especially six years and older asks, you might respond, "Your brother committed suicide. Suicide means that a person took his or her life." The child will probably ask, "Why did he do it?" Explain that you do not know, but the person felt that they did not have any other choice. Also be sure and let the child know that the family would have helped this person, but the person felt hopeless.

Psychologists who work with children often feel that it is better to use the technique of layering information. This is a method of giving small, but accurate information over short periods of time. Children have time to assimilate this information better and the person sharing with the child has time to think and not share too much information at one time. The child also has time to think about what questions he or she might ask.

Eventually you will have to tell the child what happened. Be honest. Explain softly and with great care, "Your brother used a gun to shoot himself." Or if drugs were involved you might say, "Your grandmother took too many pills. Her doctor did not tell her to take this many pills, but she took them and it caused her to die."

It is not necessary to share morbid details of the suicide, just the facts. Be careful, too, that the child is not around persons who will gossip about the events of the suicide. Children will want you to share stories and memories of the one who died. They may wish to draw pictures, write a good-bye letter to the person, or work on a memory book.

Pastors will have to deal with faith issues especially when suicide occurs. Families will often ask if God receives the one who commits suicide or if the person is condemned to eternal punishment. Persons who commit suicide find themselves in hopeless situations. They are often suffering from depression, mental conditions, and addictions. God is a God of grace and mercy. God understands the mental and physical anguish of the person who has committed suicide. We are children of God, created in God's image. Therefore God always loves us regardless of those moments in life that seem incomprehensible. God grieves with us in the senseless death of our loved one just as God grieves with us in all the tragedies of life. Families often need pastors to offer assurance that the church does not condemn them or their loved one and neither does God.

Like any sudden death, the family has not been able to say goodbye. This is especially true when the person did not leave a note of explanation. Sometimes the person has left a note and family members are able to explain to the child some of the reasons why the person felt they could not go on living. Children should never be left with the idea that this is the way we handle our problems. Reiterate to children the goodness of life and the purpose that God has for each person. Do not place blame on the one who has committed suicide. Share with the child the desperation and hopelessness some people feel when they are depressed, mentally ill, or physically ill. Let them know that we handle our problems by talking with others and seeking help. The loved one simply did not have the tools to deal with his or her problems.

Following a suicide, families must resolve feelings of guilt and anger. The pastor can be present to assure the family they could have done nothing to stop the event from happening. Most families would have done more if they could. No one would stand idly by and watch a loved one take his or her own life. Help the families to gain information about suicide and connect them with a support group.

When a child faces the death of a loved one, regardless of age or circumstances, it is a difficult time. In the years to come, the child may not remember exactly what was said. He or she will, however, remember what was done. The child will know that at the time she or he was loved and cared for by the family. The child will remember that his congregation thought of him or her or that church family forgot the child. While the adults closest to the child will have the strongest impact on the child in a death crisis, you as the pastor to children have a vital role to play. Most pastors I have known will drop everything at the news of a death in the church family and will immediately go to offer comfort to the family. Will pastors do the same for children?

Recommended Books on Death

PRESCHOOL TO AGE EIGHT

L. K. & M. Brown, *When Dinosaurs Die: Guide to Understanding Death*, Little Brown & Co, 1996

Bernice Hogan, *My Grandmother Died*, Abingdon Press, 1983

W. Old, *Stacy Had a Little Sister*, Albert Whitman & Co., 1971

F. Rogers, *When a Pet Dies*, GP Putman's Sons, 1988

D. Sanford, *It Must Hurt A Lot: A Child's Book About Death*, Multnomah Press, 1986

J. Virginia, *Saying Goodbye to Daddy*, Albert Whitman & Co., 1991

AGES NINE TO TWELVE

Lucille Clifton, *Everett Anderson's Goodbye*, Holt, Rinehart and Winston, 1988

J. Cohen, *Why Did It Happen? Helping Children Cope in a Violent World*, Morrow Junior Books, 1994

Jill Krementz, *How It Feels When a Parent Dies*, Alfred A. Knopf, 1983

Katherine Paterson, *Bridge to Terabithia*, HarperCollins, 1977

Shel Silverstein, *The Giving Tree*, HarperCollins, 1964

S. Varley, *Badger's Parting Gifts*, Mulberry Books, 1984

PARENTS, TEACHERS, AND PASTORS

Earl A. Grollman, *Explaining Death to Children*, Beacon, 1967

Earl A. Grollman, *Talking About Death: A Dialogue Between Parent and Child*, Beacon Press, 1990

William C. Kroen, *Helping Children Cope with the Loss of a Loved One: A Guide for Grownups*, Free Spirit Publishing, 1996

H. Wass, & C. Corr, *Helping Children Cope with Death*, Hemisphere/McGraw-Hill, 1983

——— *35 Ways to Help A Grieving Child*, The Dougy Center, The National Center for Grieving Children & Families, 2004

——— *Helping Children Cope with Death*, The Dougy Center, The National Center for Grieving Children & Families, 2004

Chapter Five Endnotes

1. H. Wass & C. Corr, *Helping Children Cope with Death* (Portland: The Dougy Center for Grieving Children, 2004), 2.

2. William C. Kroen, *Helping Children Cope with the Loss of a Loved One*, Pamela Espeland, ed. (Minneapolis: Free Spirit Publishing, Inc., 1996), 14-16.

3. Ibid., 14.

4. Ibid., 15.

5. Ibid., 18.

6. Ibid., 24.

7. Ibid., 46.

8. Grollman, Earl A., *Talking About Death: A Dialogue Between Parent and Child* (Boston: Beacon Press, 1990), 48

9. H. Wass & C. Corr, *35 Ways to Help a Grieving Child* (Portland: The Dougy Center for Grieving Children, 2004), 36.

CHAPTER SIX

"I Don't Feel Good."

꧁ *Ministering to Children in Times of Illness* ꧂

A child in a congregation where I served as the pastor to children was diagnosed with a serious illness that required her to have chemotherapy. During one of her many treatments, I went to the hospital. When I found her, she and her mom were going to lunch, taking a break between treatments. During lunch, this outgoing child chatted continuously. She then gave me a tour of her favorite part of the Children's Hospital, the play area. Foolish me. I thought I was coming to minister to this child. Instead, I left our visit with my spirits uplifted. In the midst of pain and uncertainty this child was full of joy and enthusiasm. I received a blessing from her. She received a visit from her pastor. Both important. God's grace given and received from two ministers, one of whom just happened to be ordained.

Hopefully, most of the children in your congregation will not have to face a serious illness. When they do, you must be a pastoral presence for the child. However, I want to remind you to take seriously any illness of a child in your congregation. What adults might call minor surgeries—stitches, tonsillectomies, and tubes in the ear-can be major events for children. Don't dismiss these procedures as too insignificant for a pastoral visit.

I remind parents often of the need to communicate when a child is ill or facing surgery. Often parents are reluctant to inform you because they believe that this is an infringement upon your time, that the illness is not that important. Let the families of your congregation know that you want to be bothered. You need to know. Sometimes, depending on the illness, you may send a card. Recently I learned that a child had been home from school for several days with walking pneumonia. Another child broke his arm. In both of these cases, I sent a card. Other times I will visit. I always visit if a child is in the hospital or has a serious illness. I cannot visit if I do not know, so I urge parents to share information with me.

When visiting a child who is in the hospital for surgery or illness, I always take a goodie bag for the child. In the bag I place items that are age appropriate. For example, in the bag for younger children I will put a coloring book, crayons, a stuffed animal, and book. For older children, I will put in the bag crossword puzzles, activity books, a stuffed animal, and books for older children. Most children like stuffed animals, so I usually include it for both ages, depending on the child. Some pastors carry a "visiting bag" with them. The "visiting bag" is a canvas tote bag with paper, crayons, puppets, stuffed animals, a deck of cards, and other simple things. Some pastors find that the items in this bag stimulate the child's imagination, engage the child in play, and present a way for the pastor to talk with the child. The "visiting bag" is not left with the child. While I like the idea of a "visiting bag", especially if you often visit with children in the hospital or if you have a child you will visit several times, I like to leave something with the child.[1]

Most pastors feel very uncomfortable visiting with children in the hospital. They are unsure what to say to the child. When a child is hospitalized, it is very likely you will also come into contact with other family members. While we will want to minister to all members of the family, there is the temptation to talk only with adults in the hospital room and not the child. Be sure you visit with the child. Children crave this one-on-one contact with their pastor.

Sometimes you will visit an infant or toddler in the hospital. Since an infant cannot talk, you might think you should spend all of your time with the parents. This is not true. You need to quietly approach the bed of the infant. Say hello in a gentle voice, calling the name of the child. Offer your finger for the infant to grasp (after you have washed your hands, of course). Pastoral conversation is mostly nonverbal. With the approval of the parent, give the child a toy that is age appropriate. You will also spend time talking with the parents and other adults in the room. Offer a prayer, touching or letting the infant hold your finger. Visiting a toddler can be challenging. The toddler is experiencing a break in his or her daily routine and may be upset or fearful. Keep a safe distance from the toddler when entering the room so as not to overwhelm this child. Adjust your height to that of the toddler, if possible, and speak in a calm, soft voice. If the toddler does not want you near, talk with the adults in the room. Present the toddler with a stuffed animal the child can cuddle with. Offer a prayer, holding the toddler's hand if he or she will allow.[2]

Other age groups of children will usually enjoy your visit and be willing to talk with you. Present them with the goodie bag that is age appropriate. If the child is going to have surgery, fear is one of the primary issues that the child is facing. Talk with the child about what is going to happen. Many pediatric hospitals have tours of the operating room and parents have probably talked with the child in detail. Your added assurance, however, will be helpful. Remind the child that he or she did nothing wrong to cause the illness.

Pastors might suggest that children draw them or the family a picture of their favorite nurse or doctor. Or draw a picture of the room. Another suggestion is to write a poem or story about the hospital stay. One idea is to ask children to write about what famous person they would dream about visiting them in the hospital. Creative children could design hospital cards.

You will want to be present with the child on the date of surgery. If possible, arrive at the hospital before the child goes into surgery and have a prayer. Depending on the surgery, you might wait with the parents in the family waiting room or return later to visit. You must always follow-up on a child who has surgery. When the child is ready to return home, consider having someone in the congregation prepare or order a meal for the child and family that is the child's favorite.

A lengthy hospital stay is difficult for the child and family. The child may have experienced fear and guilt. The child will fear the uncertain, but also will have guilt about being ill for so long, thus breaking the family routine. The child will worry about falling behind in school, missing tryouts for a sports team, or being the cause of the cancellation of family vacation time. Help the child to know that he or she did nothing to cause the illness. Discuss with the child that this illness is not a punishment from God. Assure him or her that the family routine will resume some time in the future and the family does not blame the child in any way. Talk about God's love and abiding presence with the child at all times. Pray for the child and family, but also for the medical team. As you visit several times with this child, introduce yourself to medical persons who are working with the child so that you become a familiar face to them.

Each hospital has procedures that you will want to follow carefully. If you make regular pastoral visits to a certain hospital, you will get to know the persons who work at the patient information desk. Greet them and build rapport with hospital staff. Contact the chaplain of the hospital if one of your children needs additional pastoral care. If a child has an infection, you may be asked to wash hands or put on a hospital gown, mask, and gloves before entering the room. Always adhere to these rules. They will be posted on the door of the hospital room. If a child is in intensive care or critical care, there will be visiting hours posted. Clergy are always able to visit at any time. When you arrive at such an area of the hospital and the door is locked, you can buzz the nurses, identify who you are, what church you are from, and who you want to visit. You will usually be welcomed to come back. However, there may be time in which the medical team is attending to the patient and you will be asked to wait or return at another time.

Ministry to Chronically Ill Children

We picture childhood as a time of carefree, happy, and joyful living, not a time of pain and suffering. A chronically ill child faces many challenges. The chronically ill child may have a physical limitation, a mental limitation, or both. The child, limited by what he or she can do, becomes frustrated. His or her education may have to be delayed or the child may need a tutor or have to be home-schooled. Peer relationships suffer due to frequent disruptions in everyday life. Chronically ill children have the added stress of a particular illness along with the normal challenges of development. Some stress signals these children exhibit are denial, anxiety, guilt, fear, anger, doubt, depression, and resentment. Feelings of rejection and suicidal thought may be present, also.[6]

Let me share briefly what these children perceive about their illness according to age. Ages seven or less see the illness as something for which they are responsible. Ministry to this child must include helping the child understand that he or she did nothing wrong and did not cause the illness. Ages seven to ten are not able to differentiate between internal and external causes. They might tell you germs caused the illness. While the child does not blame himself or herself for the illness, more information is needed. Giving this age child books on his or her disease, age appropriate, could be helpful. Ages nine to twelve will understand that there are multiples reasons for the illness.[7]

When you discover children in the congregation who are chronically ill, ask the parents to give you information about the disease. Learn all you can about the illness. You and the congregation can offer support when the family was involved in fund-raising projects to find a cure for the disease.

Children and families with chronically ill children should be linked with other parents in the church who have similar situations. Your community may have a network of parents or support groups in place to which you can refer families.

Pastors to children can be a source of strength and support for these children and their families. Chronically ill children will have faith issues. The pastor must approach these issues in terms of the age and development of the child. The pastor's continued presence with the child helps the child understand that in spite of the illness, God is still in control. The pastor affirms that the grace of God can be found in some rather unlikely places and ungodly circumstances. Your relationship with this child may take time to grown and develop, but over time you can earn the trust of the child.

Children with Physical and Mental Challenges

Children who face physical and mental challenges are children of God. My experience has been that these children want desperately to be included in the life of the church. Often we shun these children or try to hide them. Sunday school teachers may find them too difficult to teach and choir leaders think a wheelchair takes up too much space. As a pastor to children you must advocate for the rights of these children to be included in the life of the church.

Many of these children have already experienced isolation. Other children may have not wanted to play with them. Some have difficulty forming peer relationships. Many know the continued experience of teasing and name-calling. The church may be the one place that the child experiences a community of faith and unconditional love.

Consider the children in your church. Are any of them physically impaired? Hearing impaired? Visually impaired? Do any have Attention Deficit Disorder or Bipolar Disorder? All of these children need the help of the church to develop into strong individuals who have good self-esteem. As the pastor to children, you need to get to know these children and their special concerns. They want to be treated as normal children and, as much as possible, participate in activities of children their age. They do not want to be excluded. They need acceptance.

Look around your church building and make sure that it is handicap accessible. Children who are in wheelchairs may not be able to get through some of the Sunday school classroom doors, and you may need to move a class to accommodate a physically challenged child. Understand that the parents of physically challenged children or chronically ill children may need to accompany them on church outings. Train Sunday school teachers on how to work with children who have Attention Deficit Disorder or related disorders. These children may need one-on-one help in the Sunday school class or Confirmation Training. Bipolar children in your church may come to an event in a mania and exhibit excitability and lack of control. At other times these children may be in a stage of depression. Know the children in your church. Educate yourself to what illnesses and disorders the children have. Talk with parents on what to do if a problem arises. Always show them love and patience and never make them feel less worthy than the other children. Never blame them for the illness and never blame God.

As much as possible, allow these children to participate in the activities of the church family. In my ministry, I witnessed mentally challenged children and physically challenged children serving the church in many ways. With proper training and patience, these children can serve as acolytes, sing in the choir, help pass out bulletins, and be a part of Children's Sunday. These children want to be included in the church. Jesus blessed the children and gave them a place of honor in the kingdom. Following the example of Jesus, we bless children when we include all and allow all to have a place of honor and service in the church.

Ministry to the Terminally Ill Child

Children facing death have similar questions and struggles as adults facing death. When a child is terminally ill, we want to deny the pain and tragedy, so we shut these children out of the grieving process. As difficult and challenging as it is, you are called to be a pastor to these children and their families. Children, mostly concrete thinkers, view the world in cause-and-effect terms. You will want to begin by assuring them that they did nothing to cause the illness. These children will want to understand how God is involved with their illness. Why do they have to suffer? What have they done wrong? The pastor to children must talk about the love of God. Children need to be told that illness is a part of life and we do not always understand why. Never tell a child that God needs an angel in heaven. This is theologically incorrect and does not help the child understand the nature of God. Assure the child that God will take care of him or her. Talk with the child about what you believe happens after death. A comforting picture for children is the idea of an angel who will guide the child to heaven. These children need to celebrate their life as well as talk about death. They need time to grieve. Cry with them, comfort them, but never diminish the grieving process.

These children are facing a faith task that usually comes in adulthood. The presence and involvement of the children's pastor is essential. Children have a concrete perception of the world. The image of God is tied up closely with the character of parents and pastors. Dying children are especially observant of the character of their pastors and others. Our character gives them spiritual clues about who God is. Our involvement in their illness and dying communicates God's care and presence. Children transfer our quality of caring to God's character. Pastors who represent God to children must be present in such a caring way that children think of God as also loving and caring. Our absence may reinforce feelings of punishment and abandonment and enforce negative images of God.[3]

Begin your ministry with these children by being present. Talk directly to the children themselves. The temptation is to focus only on family members and not the child. Honest, open conversation is a significant part of pastoral care with terminally ill children. Create situations where the child can explore and express thoughts, feelings, and spiritual concerns. You need to ask parents to leave the room so you can talk with the child alone. Start at the point in which the child feels comfortable talking. If the child responds and begins talking, let him or her talk. If the subject changes or the child gets quiet, let this happen. If there are tears, allow them. Never be afraid to show your emotions with the child. Keep your language simple and concrete. Do not use abstract language because children are concrete thinkers. Ask the child questions from time to time to see if he or she understands and check for facial reactions.

Since children learn and express feelings through play, you might create ways to play with the child. The "visiting bag" can be used well with terminally ill children. Puppets dolls, and stuffed animals can be brought to the hospital room. Children can engage in role-play with you. You might bring play dough or have the child draw. Children can draw what they think heaven looks like. Children might write a poem or story. Pastors might start a story and have the child finish it. You can also play card games or board games with the child. Most important are your regular and frequent contact with the terminally ill child. [4]

Children will need your help to process his or her own dying. Help children distinguish between correct and incorrect information. Affirm that God still loves them and will always love them even in death. God will always be involved in their lives. Pastors can use Scripture and Bible stories to answer some of the questions children have about death. Give the child a children's Bible to keep in the hospital room. Read passages of Scripture to the child as you visit. Some of the stories from the Bible that you can share are:

Jesus and the Children

Jesus weeps over the death of his friend Lazarus

Stories about Bible characters who prayed to God about concerns

(These stories reinforce God's goodness and love and let the child know that terminal illness is not a punishment from God.)

The Easter story

Passages that describe what heaven is like[5]

Pastors who are honest with these children will admit they do not have all of the answers. What the child really wants from you is to know that God still cares and the child has done nothing wrong to cause his or her suffering. As we continue to be faithfully involved with the child until the time of his or her death, we communicate that God is involved, not just in the present, but even beyond death.

Guidelines for Helping Children Deal with Terminal Illness (Pastors may share these guidelines with families.)

1. Don't neglect the other children in the family. Talk with them about what they are feeling and provide books and resources.
2. Connect families with support groups and wish foundations in the community. Offer materials and books.
3. Connect these families with other persons in your congregation who have terminally ill children.
4. Provide meals for the family.
5. Ask Sunday school classes to assist with housekeeping chores such as cleaning, mowing the lawn, and watering the flowers.
6. Provide transportation for other children in the family to church events or other events, as needed.
7. Start a prayer vigil for the ill child and his or her family.
8. Have the children of the church make cards for the child.
9. Decorate the child's hospital room with streamers, posters, and balloons as allowed by the hospital.
10. Have Sunday school class members, children's choir members, and other children's groups in the church visit the child as deemed appropriate by the family and hospital.
11. Ask the hospital about providing the child's favorite meal.
12. Have a choir come and sing to the child.
13. Remember the terminally ill child on his birthday or other special occasions.
14. When you have special events at the church, bring the child something from the event. For example, if you make an Advent Wreath, bring one to the child for his or her hospital room.
15. Bring Communion to the family at the hospital if they are unable to get to church. Depending on your religious tradition, offer communion to the child.

Ministering to Children When a Parent is Seriously Ill

I had just begun my ministry as Associate Pastor when I learned that a man in the congregation has been diagnosed with brain cancer. He had two young daughters with whom I began a friendship and ministry. Sometimes I took the girls to the movies. Other times we went to get ice cream and talk. On several occasions I visited in the home, talked with the parents, met the family dog, and toured the girls' rooms. When the father died, I was invited to have a part in the funeral service. I continued to minister to the girls and their mother until the mother remarried and the family moved away.

A parent's serious illness is a time of crisis for a child. Children yearn for routine and the security it represents. With the illness of a parent, the routine may be shattered. In addition, the child often feels guilt thinking he or she may have caused the parent's illness. As a pastor to children, urge parents to be honest with children. A child can imagine much worse things than the truth. What should the seriously ill parent tell children?

- Tell them you are seriously ill

- Tell them the name of the disease.

- Tell them your best understanding of what may happen.

Pastor and parents should be prepared to have children react in certain ways depending on the age of the child. Young children will guess that something is wrong. They exhibit what child experts refer to as "magical thinking" and assume they did something to cause the illness. Communicate that the child did nothing wrong. Otherwise, these young children will be filled with guilt. Children fear the illness may be contagious so we assure them that they cannot catch the illness, unless this is the case. Then we tell them measures will be taken to keep them and family members healthy. A concern will be who will take care of them. Discussions can follow. For the young child, routine means security. Keep mealtimes, naptimes, and bedtimes on schedule as much as possible. If the parents can't handle the routine, churches can help secure friends and relatives who can. Reassure children they have a vital role in taking care of the sick parent.[8]

The sight of a seriously ill parent in a hospital critical care unit can frighten the child. Children need to be prepared for what they will experience. Pastors can help explain to children that mom and dad are still there even with all the machines. Children should decide if they want to visit. If they do, take a picture of the ill parent so the child is prepared. Some children may cry or be scared the first time they visit. Allow children to express emotions without criticism. Never force a child to stay longer than he or she wishes. If the parent is in a non-critical care unit, visits for children can be longer. Encourage children to bring homework or a game so they do not get bored. Holidays and birthdays can be celebrated as a family, if the parent feels like it and the hospital is agreeable. If the child does not want to go to the hospital, they could draw a special picture, write a letter, telephone, or write a special poem.

Guidelines for Helping Children Through a Parent's Illness

1. Talk honestly with the child about the parent's illness. Do not keep secrets.
2. Assure the child he or she did nothing to cause the illness.

3. Assure the child he or she cannot catch the illness, unless it is contagious. If so, assure the child measures are being taken to keep the child and other family members healthy.
4. Prepare a child for hospital visits.
5. Do not pressure the child to visit.
6. Critical care units can be scary places for children. Prepare the child with a picture of the room and what the parent now looks like. Let the child decide about visiting.
7. Encourage children to visit the parent in non-critical areas and to bring homework, coloring materials, or a game.
8. Secure persons from the church to help with meals and transportation so routines can be maintained.
9. Have children draw a picture or write a poem for the parent.
10. Introduce children to the nurses and medical team tending to the parent.
11. Volunteer as the pastor to meet children at the hospital, especially for the first visit, and have a prayer.
12. Spend time with children whose parents are ill.
13. Let children express feeling and emotions.
14. Expect some children to run from the room, cry, or act scared.
15. Do not lie to children, but it is all right to keep some information a private family matter. For example, if a parent has AIDS the family may not wish to share this. Most children are good at keeping secrets so let them know not to tell.
16. Be sure the ill parent is on the church prayer list as well as family members.

Prayer in Times of Illness

As children search for answers to questions of suffering and pain, the pastor to children struggles with these children for answers. Answers are never easy, especially when a child or parent is terminally ill. Children, aware that the church is praying, searches to understand why God does not heal them or the sick parent. Often adults will tell children, "I am praying for your father's healing." Churches organize prayer vigils, and children hope that the prayers of the church will indeed bring healing. When the child or parent continues to be ill, children, literal and concrete thinkers, are left to wonder about the power of prayer. Did they or the parents have enough faith? Thinking literally, they reason that perhaps they or the parent were not good enough to receive a healing. Children struggle with why some people are healed and others are not. Adults often use vocabulary that leads children to believe prayer is magic. God waves a magic wand and some people, maybe good people or people that pray enough, get healed.

Pastors to children engage these children in conversations about prayer. Prayer is not magic. This is difficult for the young child to understand. Young children believe in the power of magic and their own ability to determine the outcome of many things. So, in simple terms, we share about what prayer is. Prayer is talking with God about our needs and concerns. Children should tell God how afraid they are, how much they love the sick parent, how alone they feel, and how worried they are. Encourage children to be open and honest with God. Explain to children that we do not know why some people are healed and others are not. People who are healed are not better than people who are not healed, and they were not healed because they prayed more. We are glad when people are healed, but we know that the world is not a perfect place. There are diseases and illness. God made wonderful people called doctors and nurses who are working very hard to help us get well. Sometimes our bodies are too sick to recover and we die. Talk about God's love and faithfulness when we are sick and when we die. Assure children that they are never alone. God is with them, you are with them, the family is with them, and the church is with them.

When people at church pray for the child and family, tell children that this is a way to show love and concern. Friends and church members come together to pray, so the child knows that he or she is not alone. A prayer vigil or a time of prayer in the church service expresses to God our love, our belief that God is always with us, and our trust that the sick child or family members will feel the presence of God.

Admit that, as their pastor, you do not have all of the answers. Children respect pastors who are honest. Telling children that there is a mystery to life is better than answers that make no sense to the children. Use vocabulary the child understands.

As we struggle together with children in times of illness, we provide a loving presence that helps to calm their fears and anxiety. We powerfully communicate that the Great Physician, who blessed children, now blesses the sick children and gathers them in his arms. Now, that is an image I like to leave with children.

Chapter Six Endnotes

1. Andrew D. Lester, *The Pastoral Care With Children in Crisis* (Louisville: Westminster John Knox Press, 1985), 10.

2. Ibid., 14-15.

3. Ibid., 110.

4. Ibid., 112.

5. Ibid., 112-113.

6. Ibid., 117.

7. Ibid., 116-117.

8. Ibid., 14-17.

CHAPTER SEVEN

"Guess How Old I Am!"

❖❖ *Birthdays and Other Special Occasions* ❖❖

Grandparents flooded the cafeteria that day for lunch with their grandchildren. Since Alex's grandparents could not attend that day, Alex invited me, his pastor, to attend as a substitute for his grandparents. The more you minister to children, the more the level of trust and friendship builds, and children feel comfortable inviting you to be a part of special events. Pastors are extremely busy people. We have to pick and choose among numerous invitations. However, an invitation from a child is always special, and I try to honor it.

Birthdays are special times for children. For this reason I developed a way to remember each child on his or her birthday with a card from me.

The system I use to organize the sending of birthday cards is easy. Effort goes into getting all of the cards ready at one time so you do not have to be constantly addressing cards. I begin in November getting ready for the New Year. First, all of the children's names and addresses are placed on mailing labels. Second, I get a list of the children's birthdays. The church secretary or the Sunday school teachers often have a list. I begin to make a list for each month, putting the children in order of their birthday for the month. After the names and birthdays of the children are listed for each month, I compare my list to the mailing labels to see if I am missing the birthdays of any children. I place a call to the child's family to find out the birthday date. After completing my list of birthdays, by month, I begin to get the birthday cards ready. I prefer to use postcards; they are less costly and do not require envelopes. Religious birthday postcards may be purchased at your local religious bookstore or ordered.

Beginning with the month of January and going throughout the calendar year, I place the children's labels on the postcards. At the bottom of each postcard I put the date of the child's birthday. All of my postcards are in order by month and date and I have a reminder at the bottom of the postcard of the child's birthday. When I am ready to mail that child's card, I have the date of the birthday in front of me. A simple message is written to each child such as, "Have a great day. Hope your birthday is very special. Love, Rev. Rita."

Each Monday I mail cards to all who have birthdays that week. If a child's birthday falls on a Monday, I will mail the card the middle of the week before so the card will arrive on time. Since I have all of the child's birthday in order, the mailing part is easy. Except for mailing the cards, I do not have to worry about doing anything else with this project. Yet, it means so much to children to receive a birthday card. Of all the ways I have ministered to children, they remember to thank me most often for their birthday card. So it is important to notice the names of the children you are mailing to each week. I take time to say a brief prayer for each child as I mail the card.

As we remember children's birthdays, we let them know that the day they were born is special. Children appreciate pastors taking the time to celebrate with them their birthday. Remember to keep adding birthdays as new children are added to the church.

Children love to receive mail. I send children cards on other occasions, and I always address the cards to them, not their parents. Valentine cards are sent to the children. Be careful when purchasing Valentine cards and be sure that the cards can be mailed; some Valentines come with envelopes that *cannot* be mailed. Children are also sent cards on Easter and Christmas.

Secular Holidays

Secular holidays are also times in which you can minister to children. In doing so, you communicate to children that God is present in the ordinary times of life as well as the holy days of the church calendar. Children need a daily awareness of God's movement in all of life. This includes the daily tasks children face and the normal activities children engage in. Dates on the calendar, which may or may not be religious, are opportunities to teach that God is faithful and that God can transform the ordinary into the holy.

Many churches have objections to any association with Halloween. You will need to follow the guidelines of your church and religious tradition. I have favored programming at church where children come dressed as their favorite Bible characters. All Saints Day, the day after Halloween, gives the church an opportunity to teach children about faithful Christians who have passed away. Churches can have an All Saints Party and have children come as a Christian saint. Children can remember persons in their family or church who have died, but left an impact on the children's lives. An intergenerational idea is to host a "Trunk or Treat" party; members of the congregation decorate the trunks of their vehicles with a fall theme and pass out candy to children in the church parking lot.

If you have a church member who has a pumpkin patch, ask if that member would donate or allow you to purchase several pumpkins. As a gift to the children, I give each family a pumpkin. I give them instructions on how to carve the pumpkin using scriptures from the Bible. Often I will do this activity with the children while they are at church and ask them to give the pumpkin to a homebound member of the church. Instructions for carving a "Christian symbols" pumpkin are included at the end of the chapter.

Saint Patrick's day commemorates the coming of Christianity to Ireland by St. Patrick. You can mail children a paper shamrock with a message about the Trinity. Younger children will not understand the concept of the Trinity, but older children are beginning to learn about this teaching of our faith. Regardless of understanding, children will begin to recognize this symbol and associate it later with the Trinity.

The birthday of Dr. Martin Luther King, Jr. is an opportunity to share with the children about the issues of equality and justice. Place pictures of Dr. King around the church and use one of the children's sermon times to share about Dr. King's vision. I encourage children to check out books from the library about Dr. King.

When school begins, I offer a prayer of blessing for the students and the teachers. I ask children to bring school supplies to be given to children in need. You can recognize those in your congregation who are going to kindergarten for the first time. Say a special prayer for kindergarten children or write them a note wishing them well in school.

Christian Worship and Seasons

As the school year begins I like to offer a course for children to help them understand Christian worship and the church seasons. Children learn about the various parts of the worship service, the worship leaders, the sacraments, and the liturgical seasons. They are then better prepared to worship with the church family in the sanctuary.

Some churches provide worship bags for children to use in worship. These bags have age appropriate bulletins and activity sheets that follow the Christian year. Occasionally I will add a note of encouragement to children from their pastor.

Some of the most frustrating times for children occur when they are left out of events in the community of faith. Advocate for the rights of children to be included in any event of the church family, but make certain the participation of children is on a level they can understand. An example of this is the annual stewardship campaign. The message that children usually receive from this campaign is that their gifts and monetary contributions are not needed or appreciated. Adults come to the altar bringing pledge cards, while the children sit neglected in the pew. In addition, children learn that stewardship is an adult discipline. You can teach children that stewardship is the calling of all persons, and that it begins in childhood. Children can receive Stewardship Bags that contain materials to teach about the importance of Christian stewardship and tithing. In the stewardship bag the children have their own pledge card. Children can bring these pledge cards to the altar when the adults bring their pledge cards. Some suggestions on materials to place in the stewardship bag are given in this chapter.

The church calendar affords many days where pastors can reach out to the children. If your church recognizes the liturgical seasons of Advent, Epiphany, Christmas, Lent, Easter, and Pentecost you are already aware of these holy times in the life of the church. Even if all of these are not a part of your tradition, you can take the opportunity to educate your children about the life of Christ, which these seasons of the church year follow. Begin in worship by talking about the church seasons and the colors. Point out the paraments and stoles used in worship if these are a part of your tradition. Children are visual learners. If you wear a stole in worship, let the children touch your stole and share with them the colors of the stoles as you change them throughout the church year.

Advent is a time of preparation, awaiting the birth of Christ. During a children's sermon in worship I will share about preparing to receive a new baby into the life of the family. Children can relate to this concept. I talk about getting ready for the baby several months ahead and not waiting until the baby arrives. In the same way we prepare for the birth of Christ. We have Advent to get ready to welcome baby Jesus. If your church tradition does not celebrate Advent, you can still encourage your children to have a time to prepare for the birth of Christ. Many congregations have Advent wreaths, and they will light one candle for each of the four Sundays of Advent. I encourage parents to display an Advent wreath in the home, and I offer devotional readings for families to use in the home while lighting their Advent wreath, a sample of which is included in this chapter.

During the season of Advent, some churches display a Chrismon tree either in the sanctuary or in a part of the church. The chrismons are Christian symbols that teach about the life of Christ. Children are interested in the tree because it is not a Christmas tree, but a "Jesus tree." I like to take the older children to view the tree and talk with them about the chrismons. The Sunday school time is often a good place to do this. After I explain the chrismons to the children, I suggest that they decorate a chrismon tree in the home.

Churches can plan an Advent Fair for the children and families. The Advent Fair is a gathering where families can assemble their own Advent wreath and receive instructions on how to use the wreath in the home. Families can make a sample chrismon. The chrismon serves as a pattern for families to use if they wish to make chrismons at home. Additional ideas for the Advent Fair were given in chapter one. You provide valuable teaching when you help families link the season of Advent in the church to the home.

On Christmas Day, Christians begin the season of Christmas, comprised of twelve days. Many families are not aware of this time to celebrate the birth of Christ; instead they think that Christmas is one day of the year. Again, you can educate in the worship service. Children enjoy counting down the twelve days of Christmas. I provide them with a calendar listing the twelve days and giving suggestions to them on ways they can celebrate each day. I challenge the children to do a good deed on each of the twelve days. Children often like to develop their own ideas of ways to share. You might give children a calendar listing the twelve days and let them write down the good deeds. These deeds can range from doing chores at home to making a get-well card for those who are ill or homebound in your congregation.

Epiphany is often an ignored time in the life of the congregation. Epiphany falls on January 6 and is the recognition of the coming of the wise men to worship the Christ Child. Pastors to children have the opportunity to teach that the wise men did not arrive at the birth of Christ. Due to the long and treacherous journey of the wise men, most scholars believe they arrived at the "house" (gospel of Matthew) when Jesus was a toddler. You can use a Children's sermon to teach children the story of the wise men. Some churches hold an Epiphany Fair. Children learn about the wise men through interactive activities. Some of these activities are:

- Children dress up as wise men and have their pictures taken beside a cardboard camel.

- Children make crowns and decorate them with jewels.

- Children enjoy eating an Epiphany cake. Instructions for the cake are found in recipe books or on the Internet.

- Children play an Epiphany game. See page 126.

- Children take off their shoes when arriving at the Epiphany Fair. A treat is placed in the shoes as is done in many European countries.

- Children make treasure boxes and fill with candy to give to homebound or ill members of the congregation.

Additional ideas for an Epiphany Fair were given in chapter one. Even if your church does not have an Epiphany Fair, you can educate children about the gifts the wise men presented to Jesus and encourage the children to reach out to someone in need during this time of the year.

Lent, the season leading up to Easter, offers the pastor to children significant times to teach children, especially during Holy Week. If your tradition has an Ash Wednesday service, be sure that the children are included. You can also have an Ash Wednesday service just for the children in which you impose ashes on the forehead of the children as you say their names. I give children a Lent Bag that contains all sorts of materials to learn about the season of Lent. The Lent bag should be purple, the color of the season of Lent. Some of the items you can include in the Lent bag are listed in this chapter (p. 127).

Churches hold special services throughout the Easter season and children should be included. Older children learn from participating in a Maundy Thursday service, which remembers the last meal Jesus shared with his disciples and the washing of the disciples' feet. This service often includes Holy Communion, but may also include a foot washing service. My observation is that children really like the time of washing feet because it involved using their senses. Children learn through participation and are sensory learners. If you are not comfortable washing the feet of children, you might wash their hands.

Another sensory experience for the children is a Walk Through Holy Week event. Children can learn about the last week of Christ's life by walking through scenes of the life of Christ, acted out by members of the congregation. Ideas for this event were given in chapter one.

On Palm Sunday I encourage all of the children to wave palm branches and process into the sanctuary. On Easter Sunday, I invite the children to bring flowers from their gardens and process into the sanctuary to place the flowers in a cross. The cross has holes drilled into it so the children can place the flowers to celebrate the resurrection of Christ. The pastors lead the way and you should be included in this processional.

Parents often find it difficult to talk with children about Good Friday. Talking about death is hard, especially when it involved Jesus, whom the children perceive as a good man. We have taught children that Jesus loved and helped people. Children will often ask, "Why was Jesus killed?" Older children will not understand the injustice of the death of Christ. They will want to know why a good man could be mocked, tortured, and put to death in such a cruel manner. As the pastor to children, parents may ask you to help children make sense of the death of Christ. You must struggle with children as you help them deal with some of these questions of faith.

Share with the children that the Bible tells us that some people did not like Jesus. They did not want to listen to what he taught. Some of these people were instrumental in the death of Jesus. Jesus challenged people to change and some people did not want to follow the teaching of Jesus. Help children grasp that the death of Jesus happens because many people did not understand Jesus and did not like Jesus. The good news is that God acted in the resurrection of Jesus. The resurrection is a difficult concept to explain to children. Older children will want to know "how" and "why." Pastors should explain that they do not have all of the answers. There is a mystery to the resurrection of Jesus. You can also talk with children about other events in life that are a mystery to us. Use simple vocabulary with children. Children who are concrete thinkers cannot understand the theological concept of Jesus dying for our sins. Avoid theological concepts that are beyond the ability of children to understand. Emphasize the concept that Easter means God rules over death as well as life. Death is not more powerful than God.[1]

The Easter season give the pastor the opportunity to talk about symbols that are familiar to children. Eggs and newborn animals associated with season, such as bunnies and chickens, are symbols of new life. Easter lilies, which beautify most churches on Easter Sunday, are also signs of new life.

During the Easter season, I encourage families to plant a flower in their garden or a tree that will return each year. Children can see an example of death and new life as the flowers or leaves die in the winter and are reborn in the spring. Families can take a walk together and notice the new life in nature. They may notice butterflies, symbols of new life and resurrection. Parents can remind children that the butterfly begins life as a caterpillar and emerges from the cocoon as a beautiful butterfly.

Pentecost Sunday, fifty days after Easter Sunday, is a celebration of the birthday of the Church and the coming of the Holy Spirit in power as recorded in Acts, chapter 2. Children can come into the worship service on Pentecost Sunday waving red, orange, and yellow streamers to symbolize the flames of fire, or they can carry balloons. You can explain Pentecost to children in the children's sermon by talking about a birthday party. You can then invite children to leave the service for a Pentecost celebration where cake is served. Pastors can plan a Pentecost party in the days following Pentecost Sunday in which members of the church are invited to come and sit at the decorated table of their birthday month. Tables are decorated with themes for the month and a birthday cake is prepared for each table. Children enjoy helping decorate the tables. If your congregation does not want to do this, you can plan a birthday party with children, letting the older children come up with decorations for the tables.

Individual Honors and Special Occasions

Inform your families with children that you need to know if the child receives an honor or award at school or in the community. When this happens, send the child a card congratulating her or him. Publicize this in the church newsletter. There are some events that you will need to attend if at all possible. An Eagle Scout award in Boy Scouts or a Golden Award in Girl Scouts are examples of events you would want to try to attend, especially if the troop is sponsored by your church. These are outstanding achievements. You have to decide what you can attend, but a card or note from the pastor is always appreciated. If the child has a write-up in the newspaper, clip this out and put on the church bulletin board.

No matter what time it is—the holy times of the Christian calendar, the days of the secular calendar, or the ordinary, mundane days of life—you, as the pastor to children, have the opportunity to teach a valuable lesson about God. In your loving, caring affirmation of children, you demonstrate that God is with us in all the moments of life. All of life is transformed by the presence of God and all time becomes Godly time. In the Christ event, God broke into our time. When we break into the time of the children, we come, as Christ's representative, as God's agent of grace. What better way to spend our time?

Stewardship Bags

- Coloring papers on stewardship

- Pencils with monetary symbols

- Erasers with monetary symbols

- Key chain in monetary symbol shapes

- Children's pledge card

- Banks to place money in for a special offering

- Offering envelopes for children to use for offering

- Information on tithing

- Card "Tithe = 10%" laminated with a magnet

- Passages in the Bible for children to read or have the family share with children such as the story of the wise men (Matthew 2:11) and the story of the poor widow (Mark 12:41-44, Luke 21:1-4)

Sample Pledge Card for Children

NAME _____

I pledge to give _____
Check one: _____ a week _____ a month _____ a year

Parent's signature _____

I pledge to serve my church in the following ways:
Check as many as you wish.

_____ Attend worship regularly.

_____ Attend Sunday school regularly.

_____ Participate in the Adopt-a-Grandparent program.

_____ Serve as an acolyte. (Training required.)

_____ Participate in our children's choir.

_____ Participate in our yearly Confirmation class.

_____ Pass out bulletins at worship services as needed.

_____ Read Scripture in the worship service. (Training required.)

_____ Help pick up bulletins and clean up the sanctuary after worship.

_____ Help the pastors with chores as needed.

Other ways in which you would like to serve our church:

_____

_____

_____

_____

_____

Carving a "Christian Symbols" Pumpkin

Each person in the family should take turns carving the pumpkin. This teaches teamwork and family unity.

Note on Safety: Purchase carving materials that are designed for pumpkin carving. Older aged children can use these with the supervision of adults. Adults should crave the pumpkin for younger children.

> **Step One:** Use your carving knife to cut out the top of your pumpkin and lay this aside. Look inside your pumpkin as the Scripture from Romans 5:8 is read. Spend a few minutes talking about sin and the sins that are present in our lives.

> **Step Two:** Take a spoon and clean out your pumpkin. Get the pumpkin as clean as you can. Read Psalm 51:9-10. Talk about the ways in which God makes our lives clean. What do you need to get rid of in your life that would please God?

> **Step Three:** Use a fine marker to draw Christian symbols on your pumpkin. Use your carving materials to carve out the symbols. This may take some time so you can enjoy a snack while you work. After you finish carving, look at the symbols from the inside of your pumpkin. Read Psalm 139:1-4. What does God see in your heart? Can you ever get away from God's love? Discuss as a family how God has cared for each member.

> **Step Four:** Place a candle in the pumpkin. Have an adult light the candle. Place your top back on the pumpkin. Turn out the lights. Read Matthew 5:14, 16. Discuss ways as a family you can shine your light for Jesus and the way each person can.

Family Booklet* for Use with the Advent Wreath

First Sunday of Advent: Light one purple candle. *Expectation, hope, prophecy.*

This candle reminds us of the warmth of God's love for us and the warmth that we find when we are with family and friends.

Prayer: **Dear God, Help us to share the warmth of your love with everyone we meet. We pray in Jesus' Name. Amen.**

Second Sunday of Advent: Light two purple candles. *Bethlehem, peace, Annunciation.*

These candles remind us that it only takes a little light to make a room bright and our world bright with God's love.

Prayer: **Dear God, Help us to share the light of Christ so our world will be a brighter place. We pray in Jesus' Name. Amen.**

Third Sunday of Advent: Light two purple candles and one pink candle. Pink reminds us of the joy of Jesus. *Shepherds, joy, proclamation.*

These candles remind us that Jesus brings joy to our lives.

Prayer: **Dear God, Help us to bring joy to the lives of others as we share the love of Jesus. We pray in Jesus' Name. Amen.**

Fourth Sunday of Advent: Light all four candles on your Advent Wreath. *Angels, love, fulfillment.*

These candles remind us that Christ's light will shine in our darkness. If we are afraid, sad, or lonely, Jesus is with us.

Prayer: **Dear God, Let the light of Jesus shine in my life. We pray in Jesus' Name. Amen.**

*Suggestions: These booklets can be made ahead of time with any desktop publishing program or word processing program. These devotionals are very brief, with the understanding that families will have very little time on Sunday morning to light the Advent Wreath, and also keeping in mind the attention span of young children in the family. Churches may wish to write their own devotional materials or provide more lengthy devotionals for families with youth, single adults, or adults who do not have children in the family.

Epiphany Game

Older children can write the answers. For younger children, who are non-readers, cut out pictures of the answer and let them point to the picture.

1. What is the color of Epiphany? (green)
2. How many wise men came to visit baby Jesus? (Bible does not tell us. You can use a picture of a question mark for younger children.)
3. Where did the wise men find baby Jesus? (house)
4. What book of the Bible tells the story of the wise men? (Matthew)
5. What does the word "epiphany" mean? (to make known, make clear)
6. How did the wise men find Jesus? (They followed the star.)
7. Who did the wise men find with Jesus when they brought their gifts? (his mother Mary)
8. What gifts did the wise men bring to Jesus? (gold, frankincense, myrrh)
9. After the visit of the wise men, where did Mary, Joseph, and Jesus go to live? (Egypt)
10. Who was the king when the wise men made their visit? (King Herod)

11. How did the wise men know not to go back and talk with the king after their visit with Jesus? (They were warned in a dream not to return to Herod.)
12. Where did the wise men live? (East)

Lent Bag

1. PRAYER PRETZEL – Prayer is an important part of Lent. The pretzel is shaped like arms folded in prayer. This is the way people would pray during Lent. The three holes in the middle of the pretzel remind us of the Trinity, the three parts of God: Father, Son, and Holy Spirit. Remember to pray during Lent.
2. "GOD ROCKS" PENCILS – The pencil reminds you that God is so awesome and wonderful!
3. CROSS KEYCHAIN TO DECORATE – Decorate your cross any way you like to remember Jesus.
4. TREAT – You will find a treat in your bag. Don't open it! Your treat should stay in your bag until Easter Sunday. Lent is a time to give up something or keep away from temptation. I know you are tempted. You can do it! Remember that Jesus was tempted in the wilderness by Satan, but did not give in to temptation. Wait until Easter Sunday to enjoy your treat.
5. BIBLE READING – Lent is a time to read the Bible with your family. Take time read the verses on your Bible Reading sheet during Lent.
6. SERVICE PROJECT – Lent is a time to reach out and help other people. (Designate a service project for the children of your church to support)
7. OFFERING CONTAINER – Your offering container may be filled with coins during Lent and returned to the church. The money will be given to an organization that assists the needy in our community.
8. GOOD DEED CHECKLIST – Can you do all of these good deeds in just 46 days? Bring your list and show it to Rev. Rita when you complete it.
9. LENT BOOKLET – There are coloring sheets and other pages to help you learn about Lent.

Chapter Seven Endnotes

1. Mary Jane Pierce Norton, "Sharing Easter with Your Children," *Pocket's Newsletter*, Mar. 1988.